SEWING & SCULPTING DOLLS

ELOISE PIPER

Chilton
BOOK COMPANY

RADNOR, PENNSYLVANIA

Illustrations and book design by Eloise Piper
Photographs by Edward Kessler • Carlsbad, California
Computer services by Stephanie Gould • San Diego, California
Cover design by Anthony Jacobson • Radnor, Pennsylvania

Special thanks to:
Bernice Meissner Allison • San Diego, California
Käthe Kruse Doll Company • Donauwörth, Germany
Barbara Johnson • Doll Makers Magic • Austin, Texas
elinor peace bailey • Association of People Who Play with Dolls • Hayward, California
Judy Waters • Doll University • San Jose, California

Copyright © 1997 by Eloise Piper
All Rights Reserved
Published in Radnor, Pennsylvania 19089, by Chilton Book Company
Manufactured in the United States of America

Library of Congress Cataloging-in-Publication Data

Piper, Eloise.
  Sewing and sculpting dolls: easy-to-make dolls from fabric,
modeling paste and polymer clay / Eloise Piper.
    p. cm.
  Includes index.
  ISBN 0-8019-8872-1
  1. Dollmaking. 2. Polymer clay craft. 3. Cloth dolls.
  I. Title.
  TT175.P5724 1997
  745.592'21—dc20

96-46185
CIP

1 2 3 4 5 6 7 8 9 0   6 5 4 3 2 1 0 9 8 7

TO JOHN WOODS AND ALAN TISDALE

CONTENTS

FOREWORD

I grew up in a musical household centered around a Steinway grand piano, where piano lessons were considered essential education. I thought they were drudgery. I was expected to practice boring scales and études to acquire dexterity and strength in my fingers before I could begin to practice even the quietly simple pieces deemed appropriate for my level of expertise. I wanted to play sonatas and romantically melodic music. Sometimes I would turn to the kind of music I daydreamed about playing and start to finger through what I could understand of the score. Inevitably the result was frustrating and awful, and I hated those lessons even more.

My teacher, Mrs. Cooper, was right, of course. I needed to "take baby steps before I could walk, and walk before I could run," but I wanted to start out running or, at least, walking. Do I need to add that I did not become a pianist?

As a dollmaking teacher, Eloise Piper understands about baby steps and impatience and aspiration, but she's sneaky. She knows that if you're distracted by having fun, you don't notice that you're starting in an elementary place. She begins this book in familiar rag doll territory and then proceeds to add a new process like spattering, a new surface with gesso, a new dimension using polymer clay. She invites you to play along. If you follow her lead, she never demands more than you can achieve at any point. She gently pushes the boundaries of exploration and discovery to keep you excited about the doll you're making—even as you're learning the techniques involved in making it. When you finally arrive at the advanced doll projects involving soft bodies and hard sculpted heads and limbs, you're up and running with the challenge because you've done the baby steps and the walking. You're a dollmaker.

— Colette Wolff
Dollmaker; Author, *The Art of Manipulating Fabric*

INTRODUCTION

The Old Storyteller shown here is one of my most recent creations. She took shape from polymer clay, wood, and cloth, and once she was completed, she took on a personality and a presence beyond the physical characteristics that I had given her. That is the magic of dollmaking.

You, too, will be able to make dolls as unique as this one—dolls that spring from your own creative center, dolls that express your sense of humor and whimsy, and dolls that take on a life of their own. There is no magical secret to making wonderful dolls; it takes a lot of practice with basic tools and materials, along with a willingness to experiment, try, and try again. Like any new adventure you embark on, you must start at the beginning and travel one step at a time, developing skills along the way and accomplishing one project at a time. There are few shortcuts on this journey of creative dollmaking. Some processes are easily mastered and others take time to perfect. Remember, however, each skill you master is the foundation for the next level of skills, and each doll you complete is the catalyst for a new creation.

My dollmaking journey has been shaped by my fine arts training and a long career as an artist. I made my first doll at the age of four: a simple paper doll cut from a cardboard box and trimmed with scraps of ball fringe. Paper dolls gave way to sewn cloth ones, those in turn to marionettes. By the time I was eleven, dolls and marionettes were put aside and I concentrated on working with paints, clays, inks, and other fine arts media. Except for a few rag dolls made as Christmas gifts, I did not return to dollmaking until the birth of my first child. Then, once again, as a sideline to my career as an artist, I began to make dolls. Carolyn, Megan, and Aaron were well supplied with cuddly bedtime friends, easy-to-dress rag dolls, and carved wooden dollhouse figures. My fine arts background and ample supply of tools and materials served me well, but even with an artist's experience it took time, trial, and error to successfully complete many a doll project. Little did I know then that those early trials and errors would lead me to an entirely new level of dollmaking and then on to writing books to introduce dollmaking to others.

That is how I became a dollmaker. This book is designed to start you on *your* dollmaking journey. I will guide you step-by-step through the creative process of making dolls, starting with the basic doll pattern and sewing instructions. The rag doll design in Chapter One is so easy that even if it's your first one, you can successfully sew and stuff a cuddly cloth doll body. But don't stop at one. Make another and then make a few more! Every doll body you make increases your skill and confidence and leads you to the next level of dollmaking. Try out the different suggestions for customizing the doll body, use the human growth and development chart for anatomical reference, and add a few changes of your own. And keep making lots of doll bodies. When you feel confident with your sewing skills, and have a few doll bodies to experiment with, turn to Chapter Two for descriptions of many different dollmaking processes. Try each one. Have fun and don't worry about the outcome; at this point, it is the experimentation, not the product, that is important. You will be surprised at how easy many of the techniques are. You'll soon be personalizing each of your dolls with your own special touches.

Chapters Three, Four, and Five present dollmaking projects. Make winsome tea-stained cloth dolls and sturdy spatter-painted ones, then create gessoed and painted dolls—all these easy projects are found in Chapter Three. The intermediate project in Chapter Four utilizes what you have learned in Chapter Three and adds a lesson in sculpting with pliable modeling paste to help you create cloth dolls with sculpted faces. Finally, Chapter Five's lesson combines your sewing and sculpting experience in a challenging project for the advanced doll-artist. You will learn to sculpt polymer clay heads, hands, and feet and attach them to specially designed cloth doll bodies. Patterns and sewing directions for basic clothing and accessories are included in each of the project chapters.

To help you achieve pleasing color arrangements in all of your dollmaking projects, I have included a number of brief color lessons throughout the book. Color plays such an important part in dollmaking, both in the painting and embellishing of the dolls and in the designing and sewing of the costumes and accessories. Thoughtful selection and use of color is easy to accomplish if you understand basic color terminology and a little about color theory. Look for these lessons in color vocabulary and theory in the caption of each chapter's opening photograph. That photograph, and any others in the chapter, will graphically illustrate the lesson. You will soon be selecting colors with confidence and designing projects with original and unusual color combinations.

There is no greater sense of accomplishment than creating something of your own design and this book helps you to do just that. It leads you through the basics of crafting original dolls with an emphasis on process. Dollmaking, like most creative endeavors, is largely about process. It is not about the perfect completion of someone else's design, but rather your ongoing explorations, design inventions, and mastery of dollmaking techniques. My goal is to encourage you to trust your personal choices and instincts. I have included photographs of my dolls to illustrate processes and to encourage and inspire you, but I hope you will make your own original dolls. What better way to express your personal creative nature than through the creation of wonderful dolls! Yes, you can be creative. We are born with abundant creativity that is just waiting to gain expression. But you arrive at that creative artist within the same way (as the old vaudeville joke goes) you get to Carnegie Hall—practice, practice, practice!

While everything you need to successfully complete each project is included in this book, you may find *Creating and Crafting Dolls* (a book I coauthored) a useful supplement. For instance, the detailed section on designing and applying faces in the earlier book is helpful when making the doll faces in this book. I encourage you to seek out other informative doll books. Bookstores carry a variety of doll-crafting books as well as luscious coffee table volumes on doll collecting and the history of dollmaking. Public libraries and university and college libraries are also terrific resources for dollmakers. They offer many out-of-print books and technical crafting books as well as popular doll-crafting manuals. These side trips you take to explore new or unusual media and to experiment with additional processes enrich and enliven your dollmaking travels.

This is a book for those who love dolls—mothers, fathers, grandmothers, grandfathers, children, experienced dollmakers, novice crafters, sewers, collectors, and even the mildly curious. I hope that all will find something of interest within these pages. As with any trip to an unknown place, it may take a while before you become familiar and comfortable with your new surroundings, but do not let that deter your travels. Dollmaking is a journey that leads to the discovery of your artistic self. It is a journey that lets you challenge old ideas and limitations as you expand your skills and accomplishments. It is a journey filled with humor and great fun. So chart your course, pack your kit of supplies, and don your artist's beret for you are off on a grand adventure of sewing and sculpting dolls.

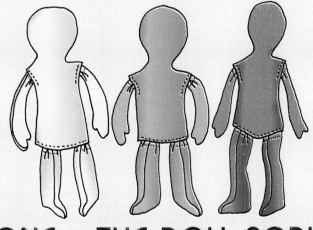

ONE • THE DOLL BODY

PATTERNS AND INSTRUCTIONS
FOR SEWING AND CUSTOMIZING THE BASIC RAG DOLL

The doll in the lower left hand corner is sewn from the basic doll body pattern. All the remaining dolls shown here are customized through alterations in their shape, height, width, fabric selection, density of stuffing, and joint construction. A protruding nose and chin and a more shapely torso are created through the addition of center seams, front and back. Rigid legs coupled with an added crotch gusset allow a few of the dolls to stand up on their own two feet.

Color Lesson One: All colors have three basic properties: **hue, value,** and **intensity. Hue** classifies a color as red or blue or green. **Value** is a color's lightness or darkness, **intensity** its brightness or dullness. Varying hues of a single color create a **monochromatic color scheme.** Here the pillows are all variations of red. They range from pink to plum, from light to dark, and from bright to dull, but they are all within the red color family. This close relationship of hues assures a pleasing color harmony.

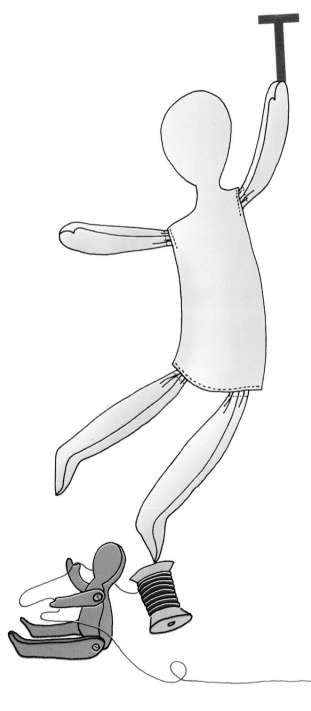

This chapter will start you on your way. When you are done, you will have made a 14-inch doll body. The pattern and sewing instructions included here are all you need. This simple rag doll is one that a beginning dollmaker can create with ease, and the experienced dollmaker can personalize to make a truly special character doll. To help you do either, or something in between, I have provided detailed instructions and inspirational illustrations.

- A complete list of the simple **supplies** you'll need to get started—fabric, stuffing, stuffing tools, a journal, and templates.

- An easy-to-make **doll body pattern** and sewing instructions.

- Instructions for **customizing the basic pattern** by varying the shape, size, length, width, and joint construction of each body component. The result? A doll that suits your fancy.

- A chart of human **body proportions** at various stages of growth and development to help you design and personalize characters of all ages.

Begin with the pattern for the most basic version of the rag doll, then experiment by adjusting the size and contour of each body component. A simple change in the shape of the head, a subtle line of stitching along the arm, and a soft curve added to the waist can transform the basic pattern into your own unique creation. Don't be afraid to play, explore, and have fun. Above all, enjoy this new adventure of combining beautiful or unusual materials with various body proportions and shapes. A new doll, one you've never seen before, is waiting to greet you. And so, happy discovery! The joy of serendipity is the true reward for any dollmaker, beginner or expert.

THE BASIC RAG DOLL

One of the most universal dolls is the simple rag doll. Throughout the centuries, this familiar doll has been sewn by accomplished seamstresses and inexperienced sewers alike. It was this doll, fashioned of silk and stuffed with papyrus chips, that was cuddled by Egyptian children. Sewn of linen and stuffed with down, it also delighted the children of ancient Greece. That same doll, sewn of flax and stuffed with bran hulls or corn silk, was the favorite of children as they crossed this country in covered wagons. And for us, it is the soft, sturdy doll that we invited to our tea parties and cuddled with as we drifted off to sleep. It is also the doll on which the enduring *Raggedy Ann and Andy* and the mischievous *Patchwork Girl of Oz* are based. While the rag doll's fabrics and stuffings vary according to the times, available resources, and ingenuity, the basic concept remains the same—a lovable, huggable rag doll.

Here are the supplies needed to make the basic doll body. I suggest that you gather enough fabric and stuffing to make a handful of dolls. Begin by making one or two doll bodies from the basic pattern, then create a few original designs by altering the size and shape of the body components. You will soon discover how easy it is to create one-of-a-kind doll shapes.

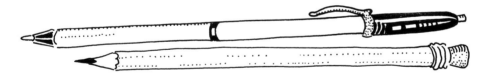

SEWING SUPPLIES

Pima cotton or muslin	Manila folders or cardboard
Scissors	Stuffing tools
Pins	Journal
Assorted threads	Tracing paper
Clear plastic ruler	Hard and soft graphite pencils
Sewing needle	Ballpoint pen
Polyester stuffing	Fine-point permanent pen

FABRIC selection for the basic cloth doll is determined by the amount of handling the doll will receive and the embellishment techniques you plan to use. Dolls made to be cuddled, dressed and undressed, and included in other child's play should be sewn from tightly woven, high-thread–count cotton such as fine pima cotton or cotton muslin. Dolls created as bed sitters and shelf standees, and kept above a child's reach, can be made from more delicate fabric; keep in mind, however, that the fabric must be strong enough to withstand stitching, turning, and stuffing.

Choose the fabric color and pattern according to the embellishments you plan to use. Solid color skin tones are traditionally used for dolls whose skin will not be embellished further. Experiment with a variety of patterned weaves and prints for more unusual dolls, or piece sections of patterned fabric with solid color fabric for underwear, shoes, and socks. If you plan to dye, paint, or gesso your doll, use white, ivory, off-white, or unbleached fabric.

If you plan to embellish the doll body with fabric dye, prewash the fabric in hot soapy water to remove the sizing. You do not need to remove the sizing if you plan to gesso the doll. Acrylic paints can be applied to a variety of fabrics, with or without sizing. Always experiment with a scrap of fabric before plunging into the final embellishments.

STUFFING comes in a variety of materials and textures. Traditional stuffing materials in years past have included cotton batting, kapok, coconut hull fiber, old rags, sawdust, straw, goose down, horse hair, fragrant leaves, and flower petals. I prefer coarse craft-grade polyester stuffing because it is easy to handle, stays put when stuffed into little fingers and toes, and is machine washable. Plastic pellets or buckshot can be used to stuff decorative dolls that need the extra weight to balance their pose.

Some dolls are stuffed with a combination of fillings. For shelf sitters or standees, use lightweight polyester stuffing in the head, upper body, and arms and a heavier stuffing material, like pellets, in the lower torso and legs. Never use a dried food product in dolls—you could end up with stuffing of bean sprouts or rice pudding or uninvited insect visitors!

STUFFING TOOLS can be improvised from ordinary household objects. I use a long knitting needle, a paintbrush with a long rounded-end handle, and a narrow wooden skewer with a flat end. The flat end of the knitting needle is ideal for tamping the stuffing into arms and legs. The rounded end of the paintbrush smoothes out curved seams, and the narrow, blunt end of the skewer is useful for poking stuffing into narrow passages such as fingers and toes. Avoid sharp, pointed objects that might poke through the fabric or accidentally cut seam threads. Commercial stuffing tools are useful for limbs with delineated fingers and toes or other narrow shapes. Look for these tools at your local dollmaking supply store, or check the mail-order ads in dollmaking publications.

A JOURNAL is a must for sketching your doll project ideas and recording dollmaking information. Include patterns for clothing and accessories and any notes you made as you developed that particular doll. You should also include swatches of the fabrics you used for the doll body and clothing.

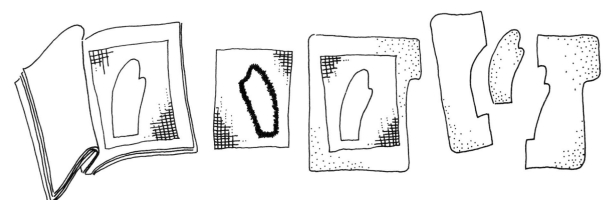

TEMPLATES of the pattern pieces can be made from manila folders. The heavy paper is stiff enough to be traced around without bending and strong enough to hold up through repeated use. To make a template, trace the pattern from the book onto tracing paper with a hard graphite pencil. Turn the tracing over and pencil a thick line along the back of the traced lines, using a soft graphite pencil. Turn the tracing right side up, place it on the manila paper, and trace over the outline with a ballpoint pen; this will press the soft graphite line onto the template. Cut out each manila pattern piece and add details, such as pattern name and doll size, with a permanent pen. Make templates for each of the basic rag doll components, as well as all the adjusted doll body and wardrobe patterns.

THE DOLL BODY PATTERN

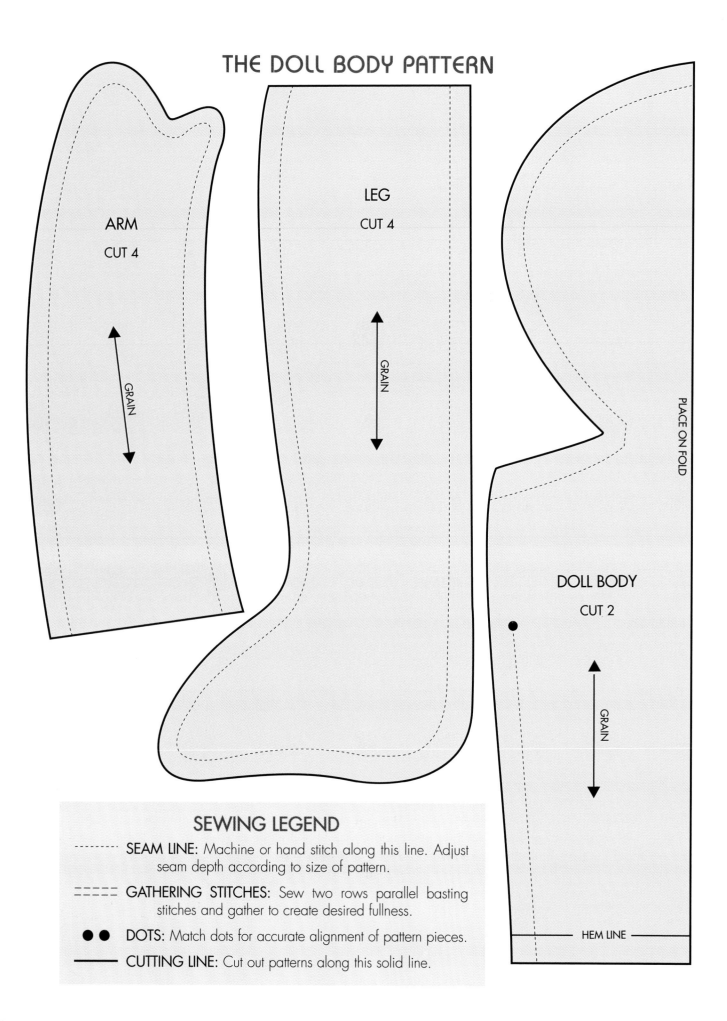

ARM

CUT 4

GRAIN

LEG

CUT 4

GRAIN

PLACE ON FOLD

DOLL BODY

CUT 2

GRAIN

HEM LINE

SEWING LEGEND

- - - - - - **SEAM LINE:** Machine or hand stitch along this line. Adjust seam depth according to size of pattern.

===== **GATHERING STITCHES:** Sew two rows parallel basting stitches and gather to create desired fullness.

●● **DOTS:** Match dots for accurate alignment of pattern pieces.

—— **CUTTING LINE:** Cut out patterns along this solid line.

SEWING THE DOLL BODY

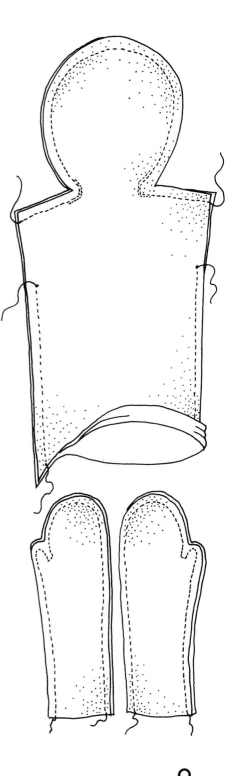

LAY OUT THE FABRIC according to the diagram. Cut out two bodies, four arms, and four legs.

SEW THE BODY SECTION. Place the two bodies together, right sides facing, and sew from the edge of one shoulder, around the head, to the edge of the other shoulder. Be careful not to distort the shape of the head as you sew along the curve. You may want to reinforce the neck with a second row of stitches. Clip the neck and head area to ease turning.

Sew each of the side seams from the hem to the armhole. Turn and baste a ¼" hem along the bottom of the body.

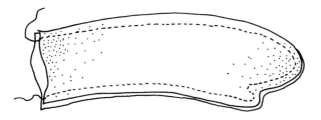

SEW THE ARMS. Place two arms together, right sides facing, and sew from the shoulder edge, around the thumb and fingers to the other shoulder edge. Repeat for the second arm. Clip curves. Make the thumbs of equal size by counting the stitches as you sew the length and width of the first thumb. Record these numbers in your journal for future reference. Sew the second thumb using the same number of stitches.

9

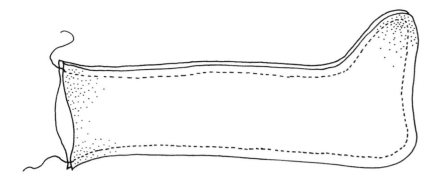

SEW THE LEGS. Align two leg pieces, right sides facing, and sew. You may want to count the stitches at the heels and toes just like you did for the thumbs. Repeat for the second leg, carefully sewing the curves to match the first one.

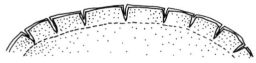

CLIP ALL THE CURVES and turn each piece to the right side. Smooth and finger press the seams.

STUFF THE HEAD and neck firmly, adjusting the stuffing to create a smooth surface at the front of the head. Make sure the neck seams are smooth as you stuff; avoid air pockets as well. Sew the arms in place before stuffing the body.

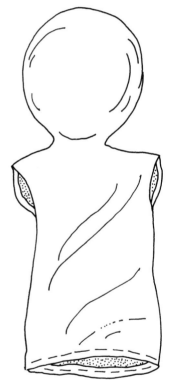

STUFF THE ARMS to within 1" of the opening. Double fold the top of the arm or create a small inverted pleat at either side and then fold the top of the arm in half. The positioning of the arm seams at this joint will determine the alignment of the hand with the body. A fold from seam to seam will allow the hand to point towards or away from the body, while aligning the arm seams at center front and back allows the hand to rest parallel to the body.

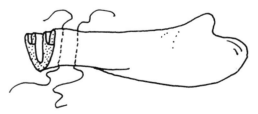

SEW ACROSS THE TOP OF THE ARM with two parallel rows of stitches, ¼" and ½" inch from the top.

SEW THE ARMS TO THE BODY. Insert the top of each arm in its opening so that one row of the arm stitching is inside the body and one row is out. Be sure the raw edges of the doll are turned under. Pin or baste in place. Using handquilting thread, sew the arms to the body with tiny running stitches, sewing as close to the edge of the body as possible.

STUFF THE LEGS to within 1″ of the top opening. Fold and pin a small inverted pleat at either side of each leg top. Sew two parallel rows of stitches across each leg, ¼″ and ½″ from the top.

STUFF THE BODY, smoothing and shaping the surface as you go. Stuff loosely for a soft, cuddly doll or firmly for a more rigid one.

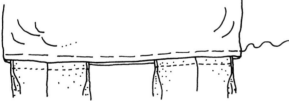

POSITION THE LEGS IN PLACE so that one row of topstitching is inside the body and one is on the outside. Baste or pin the body opening closed.

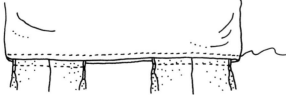

SEW THE BODY OPENING CLOSED. Use sturdy handquilting thread and tiny running stitches.

ALTERNATIVES TO THE DOLL BODY PATTERN

COMMERCIAL DOLL PATTERNS are available from a wide variety of sources. Browse through the pattern books at your local fabric store. Most of the nationally known pattern companies include doll patterns in their catalogs. The directions for these projects are usually clearly written and well illustrated. Arts and crafts supply stores and doll supply shops carry a variety of patterns designed and prepared by noted doll artists. These patterns and directions, packaged with a cover photograph, vary in clarity and degree of difficulty. You may want to read through the directions before you make a purchase.

Popular magazines often feature easy-to-make doll projects in their monthly publications, particularly during the holiday seasons. Instructions and embellishment techniques are usually very brief. Doll magazines and newsletters from doll organizations feature dollmaking projects and include ads for patterns, supplies, and equipment. Also look for interesting patterns at doll shows, toy conventions, and craft fairs.

Local doll clubs are also a wonderful resource for the exchange of innovative patterns and other dollmaking information. Most dollmakers have a favorite doll body design that they are happy to share. Clubs often challenge members to use a particular pattern as the foundation for a uniquely personal creation. Doll challenges are also presented by national organizations.

PRESEWN DOLL BODIES, stitched, stuffed, and ready for embellishment, are available in craft and sewing supply stores and in mail-order doll supply catalogs. If making a doll body seems too intimidating for your first dollmaking project, a presewn body is just the thing.

Bodies come in a wide variety of shapes and sizes. The 12" presewn doll body presented in *Creating and Crafting Dolls*, my first dollmaking book, is firmly stuffed and has a nicely rounded head. Other dolls found in craft stores include long-legged muslin figures with small flat faces and plump doll bodies with mitten-shaped hands, round heads, and jointed arms and legs. Look for dolls that are made with a high-thread–count fabric, stitched with strong, tiny stitches, and firmly stuffed. Neutral, untreated cotton is a must if you plan to stain or dye the doll body.

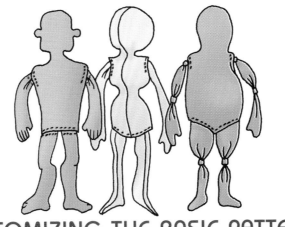

CUSTOMIZING THE BASIC PATTERN

One of the most satisfying aspects of dollmaking is creating special dolls that spring from your imagination. What fun to breathe life into your mind's imaginings, to give shape to a little character that once lived only in your journal doodlings. You do not need to be a skilled and experienced dollmaker to create one-of-a-kind dolls. These easy-to-make adjustments of the basic rag doll pattern, and a little practice, are all you need to make doll characters of your own unique and playful vision.

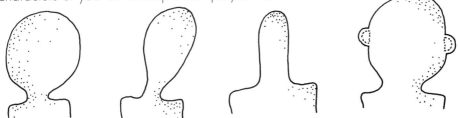

THE HEAD can be altered in size, shape, and thickness. Traditionally, most dolls have large heads, particularly babies and children. Older characters tend to have smaller heads, as do naive cloth dolls with their charmingly disproportionate figures. The round head of the basic pattern can be reshaped to emphasize the personality of the doll. A dainty young girl might have a heart-shaped head, while a mischievous little boy's head might have a square shape. Oval heads suit both children and adult characters. Ears can be included in the head shape and detailed with stitching after the head is sewn. Keep a record of these and other special changes in your journal.

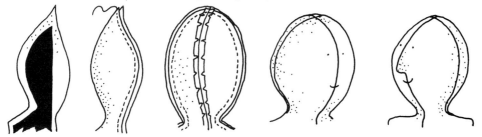

The flat, cookie-cutter shape of the head can be reworked into a rounder form with the addition of curved seams at the center front and back. Experiment with the height and width of these segments. A nose and a chin can be created along the center front seam. Place the nose at the fullest part of the curve and be sure to add the ¼" seam allowance as you would for a basic sewing pattern.

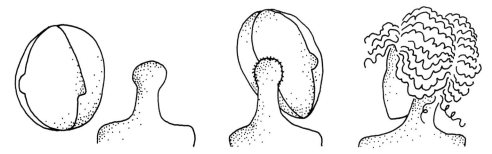

The head, neck, and body of the basic pattern are one unit. But you can also design the head as a separate unit and sew it to the neck after it has been stitched, stuffed, and embellished. This allows you to easily remake a face that you are not entirely satisfied with, instead of remaking the doll body. It also allows you to position the head in an expressive pose. Be sure to lengthen the neck or create a tiny knob on the neck as a point of attachment for the separate head. After you have firmly secured the head to the body, cover the joining stitches with a stylish hairdo.

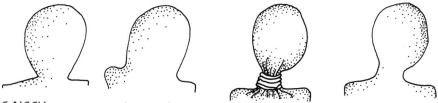

THE NECK is an integral part of the head. Its shape is often determined by the shape of the head. Young characters tend to have short necks or no necks at all, while older ones have more pronounced necks. The character and occupation of the doll will sometimes determine the length, width, and shape of the neck. The neck of a ballet dancer is slender and graceful, whereas the neck of a lumberjack is short and stout. The neck of a stylized doll can be bound round and round with cord or carpet thread, while the neck of a realistic doll is usually shaped as lifelike as possible.

The creation of front and back center seams on the head will automatically create front and back center seams at the neck. This will produce a rounder, more tubular neck that offers more support for the head. The neck is one of the stress points of the doll body, since it needs to hold up the large, heavy head, so you may need to sew a second line of stitches along the seams, then stuff the head and neck firmly. If the head is particularly heavy, reinforce the neck with an added band of fabric, secured in place with tiny, invisible stitches. The neck can also be reinforced with a small, butterfly-shaped wire which you insert while stuffing. Use a wire armature only for dolls that will be decorative bed sitters and shelf standees, **never for play toys.**

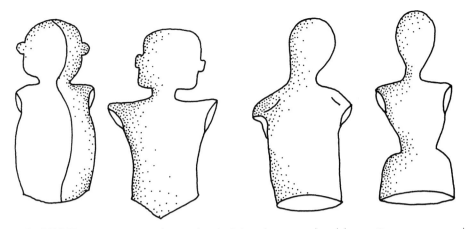

THE BODY is a rectangle with slightly sloping shoulders. Experiment with changes in its height, width, shape, and thickness. Vary the slope of the shoulders to indicate age and gender. Babies have narrow, sloping shoulders, adult men's shoulders are straight and broad, and older folks have broad shoulders that are rounded into a stooped posture. Create variations in the curvature of the seams at the waist and hips. These curves also help to define the age and sex of the doll. A tiny nipped-in waist and full hips are perfect for an elegant lady. A rotund girth helps to create a jolly old man or a chubby child.

 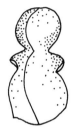 

If you have created a doll with seams at center front and back, use these seams to further shape the body. Convex (or outward) curves enhance a plump tummy and full buttocks, and concave (or inward) curves complement a tiny waist and voluptuous hips. When making changes in the size and shape of the body, be sure to adjust the width and placement of the arm and leg openings.

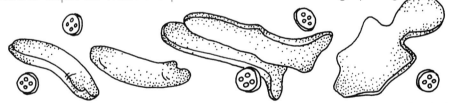

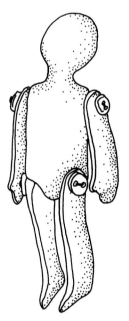

The head, neck, and body can also be sewn and stuffed without the limbs. Arms and legs can be sewn, stuffed, then connected to the body with movable joints of buttons and heavy thread. This is a great method for tiny dolls, or dolls that are to stand on their own two feet.

Most doll torsos are sewn as a solid unit, without a bendable waist or flexible spine. An interior armature, inserted in the body during the stuffing process, will allow you to pose the doll in highly animated gestures. You can make a simple armature from easily bendable wire or purchase a premade skeleton from a craft store. Loop the ends of sharp wire to avoid poking through the fabric and, **for safety's sake, never use interior wires in a young child's toy.**

15

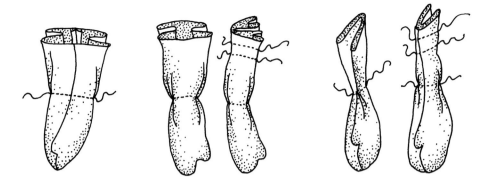

THE ARMS are sewn with two small inverted pleats and two rows of stitches at the shoulders, forming simple joints that have full range of motion. An elbow joint is easily sewn by hand or by machine. Stuff the hand and lower arm. Make small inverted pleats along either side of the elbow to prevent it from appearing too wide. Sew across the joint, being sure the stitches are placed across the area you want to bend. The upper arm can be firmly or loosely stuffed, or left unstuffed for maximum flexibility. Experiment with the alignment of the arms to the body to create a variety of expressive gestures.

An interesting variation of the sewn joint is the bead joint. Stuff the hand and arm to the elbow, then string on a small bead. Continue to stuff the upper arm to the shoulder and string the top of the arm with a bead, allowing a 1″ margin of fabric to attach the arm to the body. Wooden macramé beads make ideal joint beads. They come in a variety of lovely colors that harmonize with most skin tones. Unvarnished beads can be painted or stained to match a particularly unusual color scheme. Joints can also be formed by knotting the arm at the elbow and shoulder. Be sure to cut and sew an extra long arm to allow for the knots. Another joint is created by wrapping the fabric tightly with string or cord bindings and securing with needle and thread.

The exterior button joint is used to connect the two arms at the shoulders. Run the handquilting thread through the firmly stuffed body. Reinforce the shoulders with small buttons or beads.

The arms can be shaped to form more realistic limbs. While a person's arms come to a point somewhere between hip and knee, a doll's arms usually are shorter in proportion to its body. Adult doll characters have longer arms than children or baby dolls. If you plan to add joints to the arms, they should hang straight from the shoulders. Create arms with curves or angles if you are designing a doll that is intended to hold one permanent gesture.

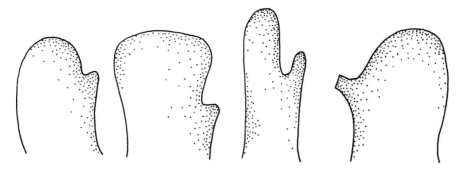

THE HANDS begin as a simple mitten shape with a distinct thumb. They can be made wider or narrower. The thumb can be short and stubby or long and thin.

Fingers can be delineated with rows of hand or machine stitching. To assure that the fingers on each hand are the same length, count the stitches of each row on one hand and sew the exact number of stitches on the rows of the other hand. Machine stitching creates the long slender fingers of an adult. Hand stitching is best for babies' and children's fingers because it keeps the fingers puffy and plump. At the end of every row of hand stitching, overcast a stitch and secure it tightly to give a curve to each fingertip.

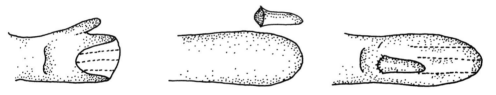

The hands can be wide with short, fat fingers and thick wrists, or long and delicate with slender fingers and thin wrists. Long fingers are useful for hands that are to hold prop items. You can also sew the thumbs as separate pieces and secure them in place after the hands have been stuffed. This creates more anatomically correct hands.

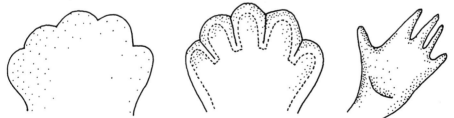

The hands can also be sewn with separated fingers. Draw the pattern with extra-wide fingers to allow for the dimensional shape of the hand. Use a tightly woven fabric and double stitch the seams, then clip into each finger area to ease turning. The separate fingers can be wired with pipe cleaner loops during the stuffing process to give the doll's hand maximum flexibility.

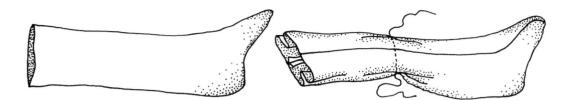

THE LEGS are jointed at the hips to allow the doll to sit. This straight-leg design can be enhanced by stitching joints at the knees. Be sure to add small inverted pleats on either side of the knee joints to prevent them from appearing too wide.

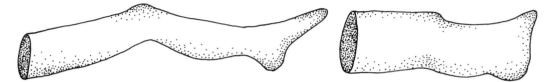

If you are making a realistically proportioned doll, keep in mind that the length, width, shape, and proportion of the leg, as well as all the other body parts, are determined by the age and sex of the character. Reshape the leg, referring to the chart on human growth and development for help in planning a doll of specific age and gender. Record this change, as well as all other adjustments, in your journal.

You can use the bead, knot, and binding techniques, presented for arm joints, to create hip and knee joints. Experiment with the length and width of the leg and try varying the amount of stuffing in each of the leg sections. Lightly stuff the thigh section for a floppy, easy-to-pose leg, and firmly pack a leg that will be exposed when the doll is costumed. Button joints at the hips are created in the same manner as button joints at the shoulders.

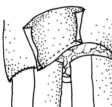

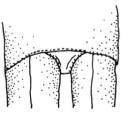

To create a doll that can stand on its own two feet, omit the hip and knee joints. Firmly stuff the legs, right to the tops, and position the top of each leg inside the well-stuffed doll body, nestling it snugly against the side seams. Sew the leg to the body from center front to center back by hand. Insert additional stuffing if needed, and close the crotch opening with a small rectangle of fabric.

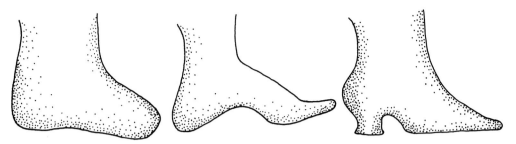

THE FEET begin as simple boot shapes. This traditional doll foot can be made long or short, fat or thin, arched or flat-footed. The shape of a shoe, complete with heel, can be included in the design if the doll is to permanently wear shoes.

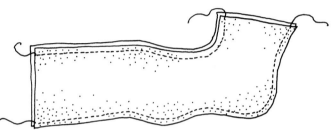

A more sculpted foot can be created with the addition of a curved seam across the toe line. Cut out the foot with a square-shaped toe. Sew the two seams, leaving an opening at the top of the leg and the end of the toe. Clip the curves and press the seams open.

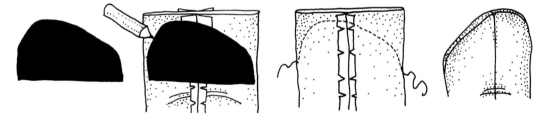

Create a template of the toe line from a manila folder or heavy paper and use it to draw a toe line onto the fabric. Position and pin the center front and center back toe seams together and draw the sewing line of the toes. Remember to turn the template over before drawing the opposite foot. Sew along this line. Trim, clip curves, and press seams before turning the leg right side out.

Toes can be created with rows of stitching, sewn by hand or machine. Lightly stuff the foot, then tightly gather overcast stitches at the tip of each toe to create chubby little baby toes. Machine stitch for long, thin adult toes.

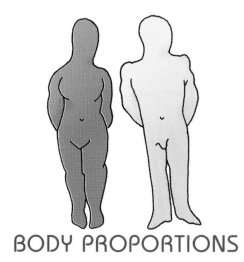

BODY PROPORTIONS

This chart shows five stages of human growth and development for both men and women. Use it to assist in the design of realistically proportioned dolls and to give an anatomical point-of-departure for more stylized dolls. Notice how the proportions change with each stage of growth. Even the spacing of the facial features changes as a person ages.

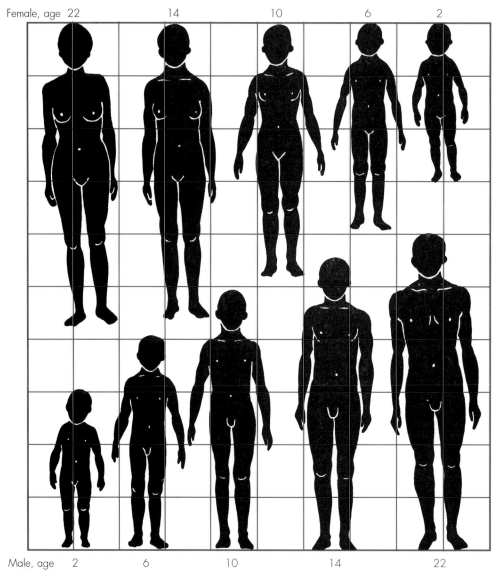

Female, age 22   14   10   6   2

Male, age   2   6   10   14   22

You are now well prepared to create a variety of wonderfully imaginative doll bodies. Experiment with these suggestions for customizing the bodies, and add a few of your own alterations. Don't worry if your beginning efforts are not what you had expected. Enjoy the little character you created for what it is and then try another. With each doll you make, your skills will increase, your confidence will grow, and you will gain the incredible satisfaction that comes from expressing yourself.

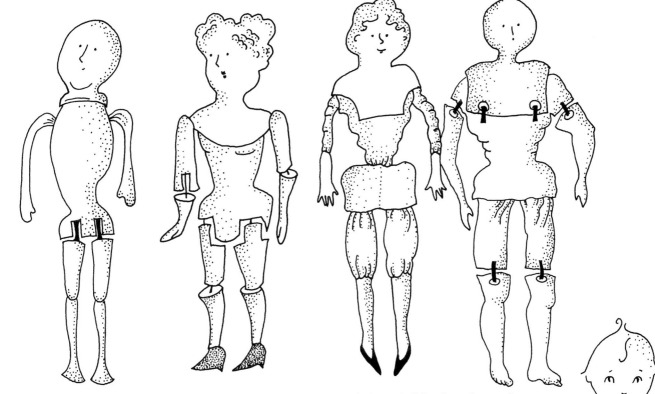

To help you get started, study these examples of cloth doll bodies drawn from seventeenth-, eighteenth-, and nineteenth-century dolls. Notice how stylized many of them are. Little attempt was made to create realistic shapes or proportions. The main considerations were movement of the doll's joints and the appearance of the doll after it was costumed. The tiny waists of elegant ladies are exaggerated as are the large heads of children. Arms are oddly short and hands and feet are miniature. Even with all their peculiarities, each of these dolls is charming in its own way.

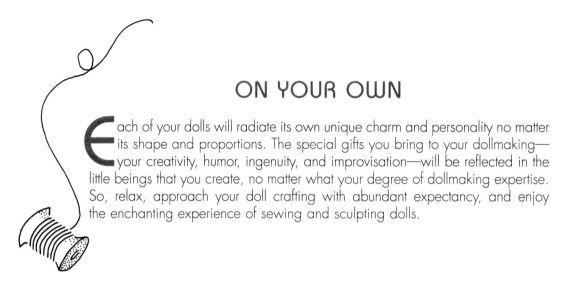

ON YOUR OWN

Each of your dolls will radiate its own unique charm and personality no matter its shape and proportions. The special gifts you bring to your dollmaking—your creativity, humor, ingenuity, and improvisation—will be reflected in the little beings that you create, no matter what your degree of dollmaking expertise. So, relax, approach your doll crafting with abundant expectancy, and enjoy the enchanting experience of sewing and sculpting dolls.

TWO • MATERIALS AND PROCESSES

SURFACE EMBELLISHMENTS AND SCULPTING TECHNIQUES
FOR BASIC DOLLMAKING

Enjoy combining different materials and processes to personalize each of your dolls. The elf sitting in the sleigh has modeling paste features which are gessoed, painted, and stain buffed. His body is colored with a thin wash of acrylic paint brushed directly onto the fabric. The baby with the pink blanket has a modeling paste face and hairdo. A brown undercoat applied to his gessoed skin areas is treated with crackle medium before the final skintone is applied. His cloth body is then tinted with a thin wash of color.

Color Lesson Two: Red, yellow, and blue are the **primary colors.** These colors, plus white and black, are used to create all other colors. Orange, green, and violet are the **secondary colors** because they are created from the primaries. On a color wheel the placement of the primary colors forms an equilateral triangle. These three colors, or any three colors that form an equilateral triangle on the color wheel, create a **triad color scheme.** The triad of primary colors seen in this chapter's photographs has hues of related colors that harmonize and accents of interesting contrasting colors.

What do you do with the blank doll bodies that you've made? This chapter has the answer. First, gather together all the materials you will need with the help of the basic art supplies list. Then try out the different embellishment techniques and dollmaking processes presented here.

- Learn how to **tea stain** and **spatter paint** cuddly bedtime dolls.

- **Gesso** and **paint** beautiful display dolls.

- **Crackle** and **stain buff** the surface of a painted doll to create a charming heirloom creation.

- Learn about the different types of **modeling paste** used to form three-dimensional features.

- Compare the various brands of **polymer clay** that can be sculpted into lifelike heads, hands, and feet.

These materials and processes are indispensable to dollmaking and are used for the projects in Chapters Three, Four, and Five. Experiment! Invent! Enjoy these dollmaking basics!

DOLLMAKING MATERIALS AND PROCESSES

Dollmakers are an inventive lot. Always have been! Iron, tin, wax, rubber, clay, fabric, wood, and plastic have all been transformed into dolls by the skilled hands of doll artisans. Even a worn leather shoe sole has been studded with a nail-head face and lovingly dressed in gown and apron. This shoe doll, found in the collection of the Edinburgh Museum of Childhood, was the creation of a dollmaker with more ingenuity than crafting materials.

Begin your dollmaking with an art bin stocked with the basics and continue to add to it as you explore new dollmaking methods. Experiment with different materials and record the results in your journal. If you find that a particular material or process captures your fancy, take the time to find out more about it. Look it up at the library, or search through crafting and dollmaking magazines. Your success will improve with quality supplies and equipment. Finely crafted brushes are more expensive but give far better control and last a long time when cared for properly. High-quality paints have more pigment, resulting in stronger color and better coverage.

A list of the basic dollmaking supplies is below. You'll also find a review of the processes that are used for the projects in this book.

BASIC SUPPLIES

Assorted acrylic paints
Liquid fabric dyes
Wood glue
FABRITAC glue
White glue
Assorted paintbrushes
Water jar
Toothbrush
Clean, lint-free rags
Absorbent drop cloth
Scissors
Hair dryer
Straight pins
Heatproof glass bowls
Journal
Pencil
Eraser
Palette or jar lids
¾" masking tape
Fine sandpaper
Gesso
Clear varnish
Craft knife
Polymer clay
Modeling paste
Plastic bags

Assorted brush-tip fabric pens and fine-point permanent pens

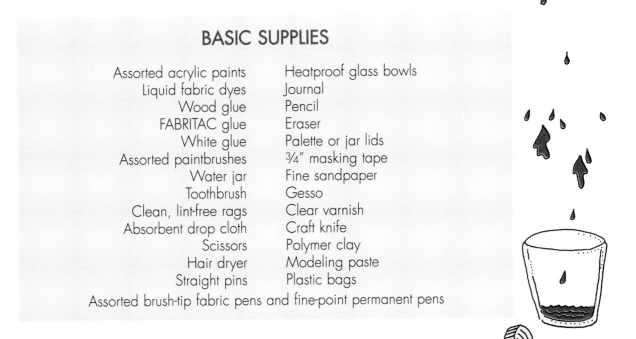

TEA STAINING

Tea is probably already in your cupboard—and this is a staining technique that's easy to master! You will be upholding a well-established dollmaking tradition when you use tea staining to create mellow skin tones on cloth dolls.

TEA STAINING SUPPLIES
½ cup of brewed tea per doll
1" flat paintbrush

BREW A STRONG POTION OF TEA. Experiment with various brands of tea because each has a slightly different color and potency.

APPLY THE TEA STAIN ON THE DOLL BODY while the tea is hot for a deep color, or cool the tea for a paler shade. Hold the doll over the sink and brush on an even coat with a flat paintbrush. Start at the head and work down to the feet. Make sure all the fabric is well covered. Some of the tea will soak into the stuffing and discharge back into the fabric. This creates the splotchy, blotchy effect that is characteristic of tea staining.

DRY THE DOLL. The forced heat from a hair dryer sometimes accentuates the blotchiness. Tumble the doll in a hot clothes dryer for a more even color or air dry and heat set it in a dryer for 30 minutes.

EXPERIMENT WITH VARIATIONS. Darken the doll with a second layer of stain or overlap the brush strokes for a more uneven color. Enhance the mottling by smearing wet tea leaves onto the wet doll and air dry. The area under the leaves will darken as the tea stain leaches into the fabric. Add extra stain along the seam lines or soak up sections of color with a dry sponge. Tea staining is a fun and forgiving process. If you don't like the first effect you've created, rinse the doll in warm water to reduce the color and try again. Enjoy the element of surprise that tea staining brings to your dollmaking—it's an historic tradition.

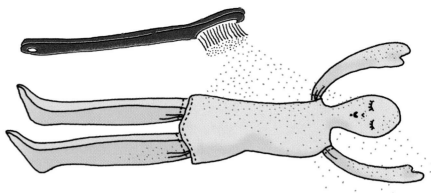

SPATTER PAINTING

This is fun! And this is messy, so cover your work table with an absorbent drop cloth, don an apron, and always wear rubber gloves. Keep in mind that most dyes are permanent.

SPATTER PAINTING SUPPLIES

Liquid fabric dyes	Absorbent drop cloth	Masking tape
Stiff toothbrush	Practice fabric	Plastic bags
Rubber gloves	Heatproof glass bowls	Iron
	Plastic spoon	

PREPARE AND TEST THE DYES. Dissolve one teaspoon of dye in ½ cup of boiling water. Dip the toothbrush into the dye, then tap off the excess liquid; holding the brush over the practice fabric, rub across the bristles with your thumb or finger. Practice until you are able to produce and aim a fine spray of spatters. Dry the fabric, check the color, and adjust the dye strength.

SPATTER SKIN TONES by layering two or more colors, starting with the lightest and progressing to the darkest. Spatter one side of the doll body, dry, then spatter the other side. Apply each subsequent layer of dye in the same manner. Always let the dye dry before touching the doll to prevent smudging.

SPATTER SPECIFIC AREAS OF COLOR to create hairdos, shoes, and underwear. Cover all areas that are to remain undyed with masking tape and plastic bags, then follow the instructions for spattering skin tones. Remove the tape only after the last layer of color is completely dry.

SPATTER DESIGNS on fabric that will be used for clothing. Place paper cutouts, leaves, or other small objects on the fabric and spatter with one or more colors. Dry, remove objects, and iron to heat set before sewing into clothing.

HEAT SET THE DYES by tumbling the dry doll in a hot dryer for 30 minutes. So it's spatter, splatter, splash—why, it's almost like being a kid again!

GESSOING

Alittle extra work—but it's a technique that pays big dividends! Gesso is a gypsum-base sealant used to prepare a surface for painting. It is ideal for priming dolls made of cloth, modeling paste, papier-mâché, composition, and polymer clay.

GESSOING SUPPLIES

White gesso	Flat paintbrush
Paint stirrer	Fine sandpaper

APPLY AN EVEN COAT OF GESSO over the surface to be sealed. Stir the gesso, being careful not to create air bubbles. Smoothly paint the gesso onto the surface with a flat paintbrush. Air dry for 24 hours. The first coat of gesso on fabric will cause the material's nap to rise. This rough surface is useful if you are adding modeling paste or papier-mâché features since it will "hold onto" other surfaces.

SAND THE GESSO if you want a smooth, eggshell finish. One coat of sanded gesso will not crack or chip and allows the fabric to remain pliable.

APPLY TWO OR MORE COATS to cover modeling paste or clay and to create a hard surface on cloth dolls. Dry each coat before applying the next. The more coats of gesso you apply, the smoother the finish but the more fragile the doll. I have added up to ten coats on some of my dolls. A smooth, silky finish is the perfect surface for painting exquisitely detailed features.

PAINT AND EMBELLISH THE GESSOED DOLL. Gesso is a slightly porous finish that accepts almost all colorants. Decorate with acrylic or oil paints, fabric pens, and colored pencils. White glue or FABRITAC glue can be used to adhere hair and trims to the gessoed surface.

SEAL THE PAINTED GESSO with a final coat of varnish or polyurethane. Gesso, paint, and sealant create a professional look that will make you proud of your dollmaking skills.

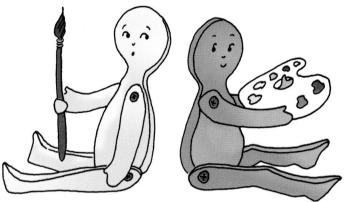

PAINTING

Be a fine artist! Acrylic-based paints are the easiest for the beginning dollmaker to handle. They are fast drying and fragrance free, and clean up with soap and water. Slower-drying oil paints are easier to blend, but must be thinned and cleaned with smelly turpentine.

PAINTING SUPPLIES

Assorted colors of paint	Clean, lint-free rag
Water jar	Palette or jar lids
Small airtight jars	Color wheel
Assorted paintbrushes	Clear varnish

PAINT DIRECTLY ON THE UNTREATED SURFACE of cloth, wood, papier-mâché, and composition dolls. For transparent skin tones, thin the paint to a watery consistency. Apply thick paint for an opaque finish. One coat of paint will allow a fabric doll body to remain fairly pliable, while two or more coats will create a harder, more brittle surface. Even the thinnest layer of paint will stiffen the surface of fabric dolls, so I do not recommend painted surfaces for cuddly, bedtime friends.

PAINT OVER A GESSOED SURFACE when you want to create intricate features. Though gesso makes a more fragile finish, it allows great control in painting those special details and is the perfect finish for beautiful display dolls.

MIX COLORS with the aid of a color wheel. Also, a beginner's guide to color theory is a useful addition to your dollmaking library.

CREATE INTERESTING BRUSH STROKES with the help of a book on tole painting. The tole painting method gives specific directions for creating a variety of decorative lines and shapes with each of your brushes.

SEAL ALL PAINTED AREAS with varnish or polyurethane before gluing wigs in place or adding trim. You are now a Matisse in the making!

CRACKLING

reate a doll with all the charm of an antique treasure through the use of a crackle medium—which is yet another layer you can add to customize your doll. Crazes and cracks can be created on doll bodies of gessoed cloth, wood, and papier-mâché.

CRACKLING SUPPLIES

Crackle medium   Flat paintbrush
Acrylic paints   Clear varnish

PREPARE THE DOLL BODY. Gesso, sand, and wipe the doll body clean.

APPLY A BASE COAT OF PAINT to all areas of the doll that are to be crackled. Use a hue that contrasts with the final color. Brown is a good base color under light skin tones; use cream or coral under darker ones.

APPLY AN EVEN COAT OF CRACKLE MEDIUM over the dry base coat and thoroughly air dry.

PAINT THE FINAL COLOR with long, smooth brush strokes. A thin coat of paint over the medium will appear lightly cracked, while a thick application will be deeply cracked. Avoid repainting over your first brush strokes since the crackle medium will tend to pull away from the primer, taking the top layer of paint with it.

DRY, CURE, AND SEAL THE PAINTED AREAS. Set the doll aside for a week before painting the features. The medium may create cracks than you had not anticipated. Fill in unwanted cracks with additional paint, then add features and other details. Dry and seal with varnish.

EXPERIMENT with various thicknesses of medium and paints. Undesired finishes could be sanded and reapplied, but I encourage you to enjoy the random patterns that are characteristic of surface crackling.

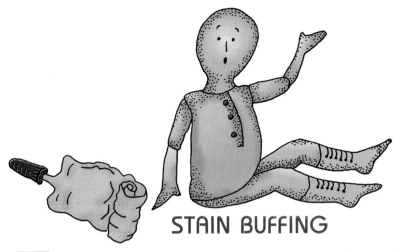

STAIN BUFFING

The same technique used to simulate an antique surface on furniture is used to create the look of worn and weathered dolls. Apply it as the finishing touch on painted cloth, papier-mâché, or clay dolls.

STAIN BUFFING SUPPLIES

Brown acrylic paint (or commercial buffing stain)
Clean, lint-free rag
Clear varnish

COMPLETE ALL THE DOLL BODY EMBELLISHMENTS. Gesso and paint the skin tones and apply crackle to the surface if desired. Paint the facial features, clothing, socks, shoes, and all other fine details.

APPLY A COAT OF DARK STAIN to a small section of the painted doll with a rag. Use acrylic paint or experiment with commercial products such as Rub 'n Buff. Rub the color into the seams and creases. If you have used a crackle finish, rub stain into the cracks.

IMMEDIATELY WIPE OFF THE STAIN with a clean rag. Stain and buff the entire doll, one small section at a time. Do not let the stain dry on any surface that you plan to buff.

REAPPLY THE STAIN AND BUFF as often as necessary to create the desired finish. Buff each small section quickly before the stain has a chance to dry. Buff off more stain in the areas that have a lot of painted detail, such as the eyes, nose, and mouth, and less in the areas that you want to appear more contoured, such as the neck, the sides of the head, the creases, and the seams. You may have to repaint and restain any areas of the doll that became darker than you had planned.

SEAL THE DOLL with a coat of clear varnish or polyurethane. There is a special look to a stain-buffed doll—a feeling of heritage and of years of loving care.

NEEDLE SCULPTING

With just a needle and thread, you can shape a cloth doll's body and mold the facial features. Experiment with different fabrics and vary the amount of stuffing. Stretchy stockinette cotton or hosiery nylon make easy-to-sculpt surfaces.

NEEDLE SCULPTING SUPPLIES

Handquilting thread in doll body colors
Yarn darners or long embroidery needles
Scissors

SHAPE THE EYE SOCKETS. Anchor the thread at the back of the head. Push the needle through the head, exiting at the eye. Run the thread along the width of the eye, and push it back through the head to the anchoring stitches. Pull the thread taut to create the desired shape, and secure. Repeat for the other eye.

SCULPT A BELLY BUTTON AND DIMPLES in the same manner.

FORM A NOSE. First shape the nostrils. Anchor the thread at the top of the head, push the needle through the head, and exit at one of the nostrils. Run the thread the width of the nostril and pull it back through the head to the anchoring stitches; tighten to shape the nose, and secure. Repeat for other nostril. Shape the bridge. Anchor thread at the side of the head and ladder stitch down and back up. Exit and secure thread at opposite side of the head.

SCULPT A SMILE with ladder stitches along the lip line. Vary the curve of the mouth by altering the placement and tension of the anchoring threads.

DEFINE FINGERS AND TOES following the directions for customizing the doll's hands and feet on page 17 and page 19. It's such a simple technique and makes a doll's dimensions so real!

SCULPTING WITH MODELING PASTE

A hag's crooked nose, a baby's pouty lips, an old man's wrinkled brow—sculpt these and other dimensional details with modeling paste, applied over a well-stuffed doll head.

MODELING PASTE SUPPLIES

Gesso	Water jar	Sculpting tools
Flat paintbrush	Spoon	Fine sandpaper
	Brick modeling paste or jar modeling paste	

SELECT THE MODELING PASTE. Brick modeling paste is a dense, white clay-like substance and is the easiest to sculpt. I recommend it for your first modeling experiments. Jar modeling paste has a softer, wetter consistency and can be shaped with fingers and tools. Do not buy tube modeling gel—it is a paint-thickening agent and surface texturizer.

PREPARE THE CLOTH DOLL. Gesso, but do not sand, all the skin areas. The rough surface will help hold the paste in place.

APPLY THE FEATURES. Knead a small piece of paste and roll, pat, and pinch it into the shape of the desired feature. Dampen the paste feature and press it onto the doll head. Press around the edges with a spoon or finger in the same way you crimp pie crust. Dampen your fingertips, and use them to further shape and smooth the paste. Air dry for 24 hours. Add more paste as needed, a little at a time, and dry thoroughly. Pages 73–75 contain full instructions, a list of simple household items that can be used for tools, and step-by-step photographs of this process.

SAND THE FEATURES and carve or sand the final details. Paint the finished head with a few coats of gesso, dry, and sand until smooth. Your star attraction can now be painted, dressed, and coiffured—and then she's ready for her close-up, Mr. DeMille!

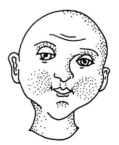

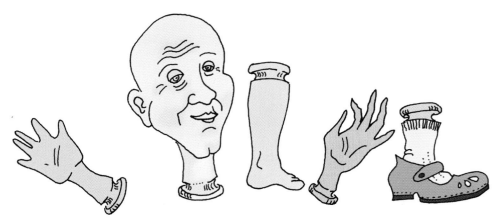

SCULPTING WITH POLYMER CLAY

Handles like clay, bakes in your oven, and produces amazingly lifelike skin tones for your most spectacular display dolls. Be sure to use a polymer modeling compound!

POLYMER CLAY SUPPLIES

Clay	Sculpting tools	Airtight storage bags
Aluminum foil	Reinforcement wire	Craft knife
Baking sheet	Wire cutters	Sculpting armature

PREPARE THE CLAY by kneading it until it is pliable. Work on a foil-covered surface, keeping your hands clean to prevent oil, dust, or graphite from becoming imbedded in the clay.

SHAPE THE CLAY using the tools described on pages 73 and 91. Reinforce delicate clay pieces with interior wires. Don't be discouraged by the instructions; it's really not as difficult as you might think. Project directions for beginning sculptors and instructions for making the armature are found in Chapter Five.

BAKE THE CLAY in a 275° oven for 20 to 40 minutes, depending on the size of the piece. **Do not overheat polymer clay.** If it is heated above 285°, fumes are produced that damage your lungs and mucous membranes. Most manufacturers recommend 285°, but I suggest that you bake the clay a bit longer at a lower temperature. Always bake in a well-ventilated room. Some artists use small electric ovens, placed outside for maximum ventilation. Warning: Do not use polymer clay if children are nearby, if you are pregnant, or if you have a respiratory illness.

ADD MORE CLAY AND RE-BAKE at 275° for 10 to 15 minutes depending on the thickness of the clay. Repeat as needed. If you are sculpting a head without the use of an armature, add ears and casing channels for attaching the clay pieces to the body after the head has been baked and is easier to handle.

COLOR THE FINISHED CLAY PIECE with makeup or fabric pens, and bake at 275° for 15 minutes to heat set the pigments. The hardened clay will accept paints, gesso, and glues. Experiment with all of them.

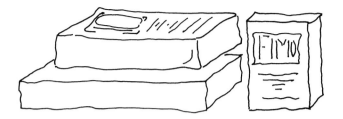

POPULAR BRANDS OF POLYMER CLAY

SCULPEY MODELING COMPOUND is opaque, white, and very easy to handle. It softens quickly, stays supple as you work, and allows you to join pieces as you sculpt. After it has been baked, the clay can be painted or stained. The hardened surface also accepts glues, fabric pen, and varnish. This clay, sold in two-pound boxes, is ideal for the novice crafter.

SUPER SCULPEY is packaged in one-pound boxes and is similar to Sculpey in pliability and texture but is a dusty peach color. Pieces of this opaque flesh-tone clay can be easily joined together before they are baked. After the clay is hardened, it has a slightly darker, matte finish that can be colored with fabric pens, paint, or your own makeup.

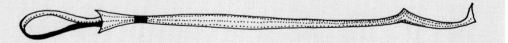

FIMO comes in a wide assortment of colors and transparencies which can be mixed for great variety. A 58-gram package is sold for jewelrymaking, but dollmaking requires the larger 8- or 16-ounce blocks. It is a very hard clay that tends to crumble when first kneaded, making preparation a bit time-consuming. Once the clay is prepared, it holds its shape for the sculpting of fine details. Pieces of Fimo can be joined together (the additive method) or carved (the subtractive method).

CERNIT, the most difficult polymer clay to use, should be crafted by a subtractive method, because joined sections have noticeable seam lines after the clay is fired. This malleable clay is sold in 500-gram (17.7-ounce) blocks. It comes in a variety of wonderfully translucent flesh colors, ranging from pale ivory to deep brown, all of which are amazingly lifelike once they are baked. Color changes may appear, depending on the oven temperature, so bake, and re-bake, all the doll pieces at the same time. This clay is ideally suited for experienced doll artists.

This aerial act features customized dolls decorated with the Additional Surface Embellishing discussed on page 39. The needle-sculpted strong man has a dyed skin tone, while the tiny tightrope walker and bead-jointed clown are decorated with sponge printed patterns. The faces of the master of ceremonies and the painted clown are sculpted with papier-mâché, while the old gypsy's features are modeled from air-drying clay. Her glass eyes are embedded in the clay while it is soft and her fingers and toes defined with needle sculpting.

ADDITIONAL SURFACE EMBELLISHING

Here are a few additional dollmaking processes. Some you will find invaluable, others you may reject, but it is the spirit of curiosity and fearless exploration that fosters your creative growth.

DYEING is the most common process for applying skin tones on cloth dolls. In my earlier book *Creating and Crafting Dolls*, dyeing materials and processes are covered in detail, including a review of brands and color selections, and directions for allover dyeing, sectional dyeing, and machine dyeing. Even though the information is not repeated in this book, include all three dyeing methods in your dollmaking repertoire.

SPONGE PAINTING with dyes or paints and a kitchen sponge produces interesting textural effects. Overlap various colors, drying each before adding the next, or try different sponges for a variety of textures.

STAMP PRINTING is a fun way to create patterns on the doll's body and clothing. Carve your own designs into white erasers or use sponge shapes, cardboard cutouts, corks, or commercial stamps. Be sure to print with waterproof ink or paint, and heat set the dried colors in a hot clothes dryer.

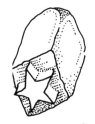

SPRAY PAINTING with aerosol cans of paint colors the doll body with a very even layer of pigment. Spray varnishes, adhesives, and primers are also available. Use an airbrush to create the same even effect, blend rosy cheeks, and form crisply painted hairdos.

MODELING WITH PAPIER-MÂCHÉ is much the same as sculpting with modeling paste. Papier-mâché is lightweight and less fragile than modeling paste and accepts almost all embellishments.

SCULPTING WITH AIR-DRYING CLAYS omits the need for an oven to set the material. There are a variety of air-drying clays, each with its own texture. Experiment with them until you find one you prefer.

ON YOUR OWN

You now have all the supplies and information you need to make a lot of dolls. Use the doll bodies you have made to experiment with the different embellishment techniques. Don't be timid about trying processes that are unfamiliar. Some of your most interesting dolls will take shape from experimentation and happy accident. I believe there is no such thing as a mistake—an unplanned result is merely an opportunity to try out a creative alternative.

THREE • PLAIN AND FANCY DOLLS

EASY-TO-MAKE CLOTH DOLLS USING
THE BASIC DOLL BODY PATTERN

Make a tea-stained Plain Amish Doll from the basic doll body pattern, then create spatter-painted Play Pals using some of the customizing suggestions. Next create Fancy Dolls that combine customized doll bodies with gessoed and painted skin tones. The amount of stuffing will affect the pose of each doll. Solidly stuffed, unjointed limbs remain rigid while unstuffed upper arms are flexible and easy to pose. The tiny dolls are customized variations of the Plain and Fancy Dolls. The freshly laundered clothing was sewn from the Basic Wardrobe Patterns.

Color Lesson Three: A **split triad color scheme** combines two colors from a triad with one color that is not part of the triad. For example, red and blue are part of the primary triad of red, blue, and yellow. When violet, which is not in the primary triad, is used with red and blue, a split triad color arrangement is created. This color scheme has the harmony of colors that share a common hue (blue and violet, and red and violet) plus the interesting contrast of dissimilar hues (red and blue). A few colors used in varying amounts are more pleasing than many random hues.

Here are some delightful, easy-to-make projects to start you on your dollmaking journey. You will combine the cloth doll bodies from Chapter One with some of the embellishment techniques from Chapter Two for a variety of imaginative characters.

Each of these doll projects represents a traditional dollmaking technique. Begin with the quick-and-easy Plain Amish Children, and you'll soon progress to the more challenging Fancy Dolls. Create an entire wardrobe for each doll from the basic wardrobe patterns and sewing instructions at the end of each chapter.

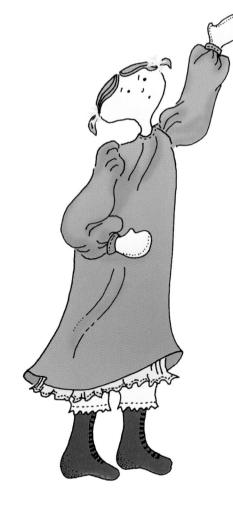

- Transform your first rag doll bodies into adorable **Plain Amish Children.** These cuddly, tea-stained Amish children and their perky, spatter-painted **Play Pals** will delight children of all ages.

- Develop your painting skills by creating a variety of **Fancy Dolls.** Gesso and paint a few enchanting characters, then add hairdos made from fur and recycled wigs. Here's a chance to express your sense of beauty and whimsy!

- Costume each doll in an imaginative outfit using the basic **wardrobe patterns** as a starting point.

Each of the projects is designed to encourage you to creatively explore the various materials and processes and make your dollmaking experience successful.

PLAIN AMISH CHILDREN

Plain Dolls are just plain easy to make! Create these winsome little Plain Amish Children from the basic rag doll body, a traditional skin tone embellishment, and an easy-to-apply face and hair design. Sew the Amish plain dress from the basic wardrobe pattern pieces, using the help of the easy-to-follow sewing instructions at the end of the chapter.

The charm of these Plain Dolls is their timeless simplicity, which begins with a soft skin tone created from a stain of brewed tea. Tea has been a traditional colorant for creating the skin tones of cloth dolls for centuries. In times and places when commercial dyes were not readily available, women colored fabrics, yarns, and threads with pigments extracted from easy-to-find natural substances. Onion skins were used to produce a bright yellow coloring, walnut hulls were transformed into dark brown dye, and polkberry juice was turned into a deep red stain. A strong brew of tea was used to produce a range of colors from warm ivory to rich brown. This method produced the skin tones of many homemade cloth dolls, as well as the delicate ivory tints on gloves, hankies, and the lace trim of fine gowns.

You can create a wonderful array of skin tones on your dolls by using this time-honored method, transforming white fabric into tints of pale tan and turning unbleached muslin into warm ivories or soft golden browns. Tea staining is also the ideal method for creating clothing that looks authentically yellowed with age and for antiquing lace and other trims to match that special outfit.

These adorable dolls are so easy and so much fun to make that you will want to construct an entire family. So stitch up a few doll bodies and go to it!

PLAIN AMISH CHILDREN SUPPLIES

Basic rag doll body   Large-eyed needle
½ cup tea per doll   Scissors and straight pins
1" flat paintbrush   Clean, lint-free rag
Assorted brush-tip fabric pens and fine-point permanent pens
Embroidery floss for hair, mouth, and nose

TEA STAIN THE DOLL BODY. Experiment with the various tea staining methods described on page 28. Try a variety of tea brands to create different tints. I prefer Earl Grey bulk tea in a potent brew; it creates a deep, warm tan color. Record the processes you use in your journal.

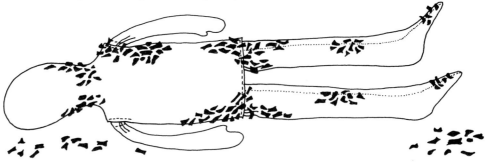

ADD EXTRA SPLOTCHES by sprinkling the wet tea leaves over the wet, tea-stained body and set the doll aside to air dry. The tea leaves will leach more pigment onto the fabric, creating a highly textured stain.

Tea staining is a very forgiving medium. If you don't like the first effect you've created, darken the doll with another layer of stain or rinse the doll in warm water to reduce the intensity of the color. Enjoy the element of surprise that comes with the change in coloration as the doll body dries. Those splotches and blotches of uneven stain, part of the charm of the tea-stained dolls our great-grandmothers made, will also give character and charm to your first dollmaking efforts.

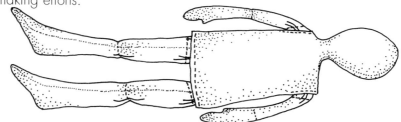

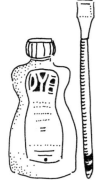

HEAT SET THE DOLL BODY by tumbling it in a hot clothes dryer for 30 minutes. This will prevent the color from rubbing off; however, the fugitive nature of tea stain will not allow for a vigorous machine washing. I suggest you try a commercial dye applied in the same manner as tea stain for dolls that are to be the washable companions of young children. Be sure to enter the dye recipe in your journal.

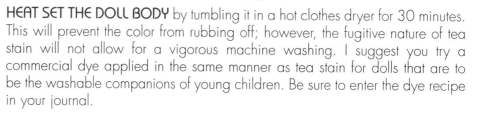

DESIGN A SIMPLE LINE AND DOT FACE. It is amazing how many different faces you can create from two dots for eyes and curved lines for a nose and a mouth. Practice drawing faces in your journal. Vary the size of each feature and alter the distances between them. The relationship of size and placement of these simple features can create an unlimited variety of expressions.

Think of the eyes, nose, and mouth as a single unit and adjust it to fit the head size and personality of your doll character. Remember to leave room for a forehead and chin. Young children have large foreheads and full cheeks, while adults have larger chins and longer noses. If the doll is to have whiskers, increase the space between the nose and mouth to allow for the added embellishments.

POSITION THE FEATURES on the doll head. Mark the eye placement by sticking straight pins into the head. Use a small piece of sewing thread to lay out a smile. You can fine-tune the expression by repositioning the straight pin eyes and recurving the thread mouth. The pinholes at unwanted locations are easily removed with a gentle rub of the finger.

DRAW THE EYES with a black fine-point permanent pen. Trace around the pinheads, remove the pins, and fill in the small circles with the pen. Try experimenting with simple variations of the basic dot. Create a highlight in each eye by omitting the ink from a pie-shaped wedge. Add upper or lower lashes or curved eyebrows to further define the eyes. A small ring of iris color around the black pupil, applied with a brush-tip fabric pen, will add a bit more color to the face.

EMBROIDER THE NOSE AND MOUTH. A few overcast stitches are all you need for the nose. The mouth is created from a curved line of tiny backstitches. These features can also be drawn with a brown fine-point permanent pen, then shaded with a peach brush-tip fabric pen.

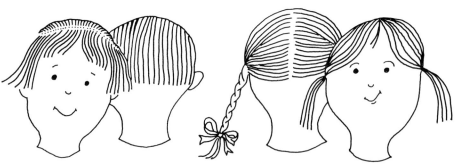

ADD A HAIRDO OF EMBROIDERY FLOSS. Use a modified satin stitch to cover the crown of the head. Anchor strands of floss at the front of the hairline for bangs and at the sides of the head for braids.

A BLUSH ON THE CHEEKS is an optional finishing touch. Lightly apply a peach-colored blush with the side of a brush-tip fabric pen or smooth a bit of acrylic paint on each cheek with a soft cloth using a light swirling motion. Rub in the same motion, with a clean rag, to remove any excess pigment. It takes some practice to achieve a light tint of color, so blush some scrap fabric before blushing your doll.

YOU'RE DONE! Now that you have completed your first Plain Doll, why not make another one! Vary the body shape, the face design, and the hairdo. And then it's time to dress your dolls. Basic clothing patterns and sewing instructions, found at the end of this chapter, can be customized to form an unlimited variety of clothes and are the foundation for all the costumes in this book.

The black bonnets, aprons, and vest add a touch of authenticity to the Plain Amish Dolls' clothing and provide a striking contrast to the pastel shades of rose, pink, lavender, and soft blue. The boy's wide-brimmed hat is created from a purchased felt cowboy hat. The crown of the hat is dampened and reshaped into the dome of the Amish hat, and the brim is set sideways on the doll's head to appear wider. The vest pattern is found in Chapter Four's Wardrobe Accessories, and the bonnet pattern is in Chapter Five's Finishing Touches.

PLAY PALS

Another uncomplicated Plain Doll, one that combines a traditional decorative technique with a simple face and hairdo, is the spatter-painted Play Pal. This is an easy project for the beginning dollmaker and is based on the ancient technique of resist. Spatter painting is one of several methods for applying design to fabric by blocking out certain areas of the material and coloring other sections with dyes or paint. It is believed that over 35,000 years ago primitive artisans pressed the juice from berries through insect-chewed leaves to create the first decorative resist patterns. Stencil art, batik, spatter paint, ikat, and tie-dye are a few of the art forms that spring from this early decorative method.

Spatter painting is a fun and versatile technique for your dollmaking. It can be used to create allover colors for skin tones and specific areas of color for hair, underwear, and stockings. It can also be used to decorate fabric for the doll's wardrobe and accessories. You can apply it before the doll body is sewn or after the doll has been sewn and stuffed. I recommend the latter for your first efforts. To begin, sew a doll body or two. Why not try out a few of the suggestions on pages 13–19 for customizing each doll? I've added ears and big feet to some of my Play Pals, needle sculpted the hands of some, and changed the head shape to give each doll a unique personality.

Now you're ready to spatter paint the embellishments. It's so easy to do that the young children in your life can participate in the fun of dollmaking as they share in the creation of a passel of Play Pals.

PLAY PAL SUPPLIES

Basic doll body	Plastic bags	Embroidery floss
Practice fabric	Toothbrush	Large-eyed needle
Liquid fabric dye	Scissors	Heatproof glass bowls
Masking tape	Straight pins	Absorbent drop cloth

Assorted brush-tip fabric pens and fine-point permanent pens

PLAN THE DOLL by sketching a few designs in your journal. Include painted underwear and stockings in some of the sketches, then design others with unpainted clothing. The easiest dolls to make are ones with colored clothing. Once you have created a few dolls using this overlapping method of applying color, experiment with blocking out sections on unpainted doll bodies to create white clothing and stockings.

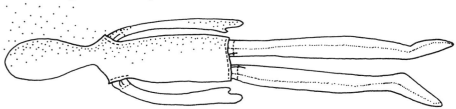

SPATTER PAINT THE SKIN TONE. Dolls with colored underwear begin with an allover skin color, from head to foot. Skin tones are created by blending together two or more layers of color for a speckled, freckled look. The directions for spatter painting are presented on page 29. Practice on a scrap of doll body fabric before spattering on the actual doll body. Remember, spatter painting is messy, so wear rubber gloves and cover the work surface with an absorbent drop cloth. Avoid newspapers because the ink tends to rub off on hands, equipment, and the dolls.

Apply one layer of color at a time, beginning with the lightest and progressing to the darkest. Dry each layer thoroughly before touching the doll or adding the next layer of color. Combinations of yellow and orange, yellow and tan, orange and red, red and tan, tan and brown, and even orange and lavender make marvelous skin tones.

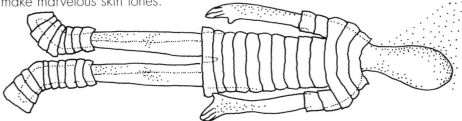

TRY CREATING SOME DOLLS WITH UNPAINTED UNDERWEAR and stockings. Cover the areas that are to remain undyed with masking tape. Press the tape firmly in place, then follow the instructions for spatter painting the skin tones. Remove the tape only after the last layer of color is completely dry.

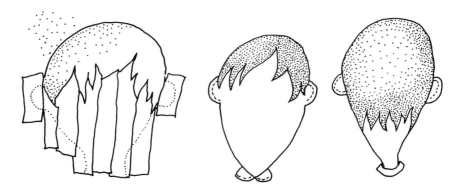

SPATTER PAINT THE HAIRDO. To mask out areas on the doll that you don't want to dye, cover the doll body by placing it into a plastic bag. Gather and tape the bag around the neck. Cover the remaining areas of the face, ears, and the back of the neck with strips of masking tape, cutting out the areas that will define the ends of the hair. Spatter the layers of color onto the unmasked section of the head. Dry each coat before applying the next. Remove the tape after the final coat has thoroughly dried.

SPATTER PAINT THE UNDERWEAR. Mask out all but the underwear section on the doll body with tape and plastic bags. Build up layers of color to define the clothing, drying each layer before adding the next.

APPLY A SIMPLE FACE using the same dot-and-line design that you used for the Plain Amish Children. A touch of needle sculpting, explained on page 34, adds dimension to the eyes. Anchor the stitches at the side seams rather than the back of the head to make them less conspicuous.

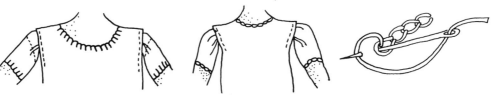

EMBROIDER THE TRIM around the edges of the underwear. A simple chain or buttonhole stitch makes a lovely finishing detail. Create a snazzy outfit from the patterns at the end of the chapter.

GOOD JOB! You have now finished the Plain Dolls. Be sure to enter all pertinent information in your journal. Did you vary the skin tone for each doll and experiment with different expressions? Did you have fun? Do you want to learn more? Create another and then another, developing your skills as you go. You will soon be able to make the exact doll that lives in your mind's eye.

Adjust the basic clothing patterns to make an unlimited variety of garments for your dolls. These Play Pals have been dressed in colorful outfits cut from the jumper, shirt, and pants patterns. Decorative trims and notions add perky accents to each outfit. An old embroidered handkerchief, found at a thrift store, is transformed into the seated doll's dainty apron. The boy's beanie is sewn from reworked pattern sections of the doll's head and trimmed with a large flower-shaped button—another thrift store treasure.

FANCY DOLLS

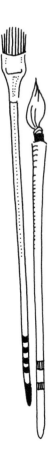

Fancy Dolls challenge the novice dollmaker with a more complex combination of embellishment techniques. The skin areas of the doll body are sealed with a few layers of gesso, sanded, then painted with one or more coats of skin tone. The features are painted, and the doll is sealed with a clear varnish. Hair is fashioned of fur or recycled wigs and glued in place after the varnish is dry. Areas of underwear remain unpainted and are trimmed with embroidery. And then comes the reward for your work—the opportunity to dress each doll in your most imaginative, fancy costume.

Gesso, a solution of gypsum, glue, and whitening in a water-soluble base, is a sealant for wood, fabric, and paper. It was used to prepare the wooden triptychs of medieval church art, the stretched painting canvases from Renaissance to the present, and the intricate wood carvings of Baroque and Rococo furnishings. Gesso has also been used as a dollmaking material for centuries. Sixteenth-century wooden peg dolls were often gessoed before they were painted. Seventeenth-century papier-mâché doll heads were coated before they were embellished, as were many composition and cloth dolls of the eighteen hundreds and nineteen hundreds. Today, gesso continues to be a mainstay for artists, artisans, and of course dollmakers.

Gessoed surfaces are easy to paint and can be sanded down and repainted if you are not pleased with your first efforts. Gessoed and painted Fancy Dolls will tickle your fancy, advance your dollmaking skills, and allow you to create a very special doll.

FANCY DOLL SUPPLIES

Firm doll body	Water jar
Practice fabric	Palette
White gesso	Hard graphite pencil
Fine sandpaper	Embroidery floss
Clean, lint-free rag	FABRITAC glue
Paintbrushes	Clear varnish
Assorted paints	Small piece of fur or wig

Assorted brush-tip fabric pens and fine-point permanent pens

PLAN AND PREPARE THE DOLL

Draw a number of characters in your journal. Let your imagination soar! Inspiration can be culled from fairy tales, folklore and other favorite literature, old family photographs, history, and various world cultures—to name just a few sources. Customize the shape and size of the doll to suit the personality of the character you have chosen.

SEW THE DOLL BODY to conform to your sketches, then firmly stuff the body. If your first effort is not quite the doll you had envisioned, rework the pattern pieces and sew another one, saving the first doll body for another project.

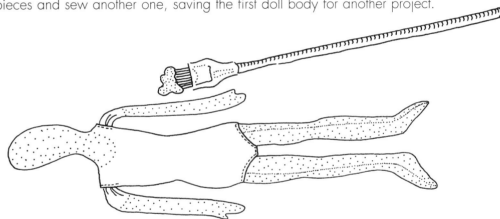

GESSO ALL THE SKIN AREAS following the directions on page 30. Unpainted areas become the underwear. Apply one to five thin layers, drying each coat before applying the next. After the final layer is dry, sand the gesso until it is a smooth, eggshell texture. Wipe off the chalky dust with a clean, lint-free rag.

PAINT THE SKIN TONE. Mix the skin color in a small jar with a watertight lid. Mix enough paint for at least two layers on all skin areas, plus a tablespoon or so for future color mixing and touch-ups. Apply two coats, drying the first before painting the second.

OPTIONAL VARIATIONS of the Fancy Dolls include a variety of antique finishes. Use acrylic crackling medium to create the look of cracked and peeling paint, or apply a buffed stain for an aged and worn surface. The directions for these methods are found on pages 32–33.

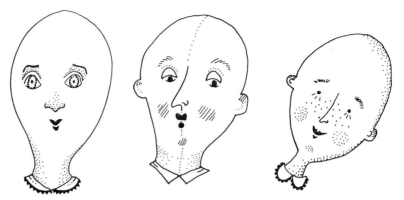

PAINT THE FACE, HANDS, AND FEET

Begin by adjusting the face you drew in your journal to fit the actual size and contour of the cloth head. Redraw the features to scale, and cut out templates for the eye and mouth shapes. Lightly trace the templates onto the doll head with a hard graphite pencil. Remember to flip the eye template over for the second eye to create a mirror image of the first. If you need to reposition a feature after you have drawn it, paint over the unwanted lines with the skin tone paint and then redraw it.

OUTLINE THE MAIN FEATURES with a brown fine-point permanent pen. Draw the eyes, nose, and mouth, emphasizing the upper eye lids, the tip of the nose, and the center line of the lips. These dominant lines of the face most define the expression. Don't make too detailed a drawing. A simple face, drawn with a few well-placed lines, is often more effective than a very detailed one. Save the details such as eyelashes and eyebrows until you have painted the basics.

PAINT THE EYES. Fill in the white areas with two coats of paint and let dry. Draw the pupils with a black fine-point permanent pen. Paint the irises and add a bit of detail to each by painting dots of a deeper color around the rims. Paint a pink dot at the inside corner of each eye, and add a sparkle to the iris with a dot of white. Darken a dab of the skin paint with a touch of brown and paint small upper eyelids.

PAINT THE MOUTH. Add a bit of red or peach to the skin color paint. Paint the upper lip. Lighten this lip shade with white paint and paint the bottom lip. Add a highlight of light pink to the lower lip. Refresh any smudged pen lines.

MIX A BLUSH COLOR by adding a touch of red to a small amount of the skin tone color. Mix enough to shade the nose, cheeks, hands, and feet.

PAINT THE NOSE. Blend the blush color from the tip of the nose to the bridge with a clean, dry brush. Further define the nose with a darker shade of the blush color, directly above the tip of the nose.

BLUSH THE CHEEKS with small circles of color. Blend the edges of each circle into the skin tone for a softer effect.

PAINT THE HANDS. Tint the palms, knuckles, and fingertips with blush color. Add a few lines of darkened skin color to define the fingers.

PAINT THE FEET with a tint of blush at the toe tips, heels, and soles. Or develop your painting skills by painting a shoe design. Lace the painted shoes with a crisscross of actual embroidery floss and tie in a bow. Put a drop of glue on the center of the bow to prevent it from coming untied.

ADD A FEW DETAILS to complete the doll. Paint eyebrows and lashes with fine, hairlike strokes, or draw the brows and lashes with a fine-point permanent pen. I like to combine strokes of black and brown for a natural look. You can also add ribbing along the sock tops, a few simple details on the painted shoes, or fingernails on the hands.

VARNISH THE FACE, HANDS, AND FEET with clear varnish or polyurethane.

CONGRATULATIONS! You have now completed a Fancy Doll. What kind of little person is looking back at you, waiting for a hairdo and an outfit? Do you have a solemn little girl, a chubby old man, or long-legged school chum? Will your doll wear a fancy Sunday-Go-to-Meeting outfit or practical roughhouse clothes? Use the costume sketches from your journal to customize the basic clothes patterns.

CREATING A WIG

Craft a doll wig for your Fancy Doll from an old mink coat collar, a dyed fox cuff, a worn-out sheepskin seat cover, or that old wig of yours that has been gathering dust in the closet since 1965.

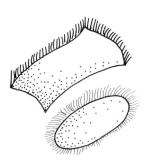

MINK COLLAR CREW CUTS are the perfect toppers for little boy dolls. Cut out a paper oval or rectangle, place it on the doll's head, and adjust it to fit. Trace the pattern onto the back of a piece of fur. Cut through the foundation layer with a craft knife or sharp scissors. Do not cut into the hairs; they will automatically separate after you have made the cut. Glue the wig in place. Conceal the edges of the wig by covering them with additional fur. Use a toothpick to spread a line of glue around the doll's head directly at the edge of the wig. Press the fur edge into the glue.

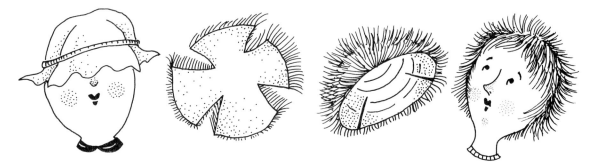

LOCKS OF FOX AND SHEEPSKIN SHAGS make perfect schoolgirl hairdos. Fit a paper towel over the doll's head, and secure it with a rubber band. Finger press the folds to form four small darts at an equal distance from the center, front and back, of the head. Mark and trim the hairline, remove the pattern from the doll's head, and clip the darts to form notches. Trace the pattern onto the fur hide. Cut out the wig, glue or whipstitch the notches closed, then glue the wig in place. Cover the leather edge by folding it under and securing it with glue, or glue the fur along the edge of the wig onto the doll's head.

GRISLY BEARDS, BUSHY EYE BROWS, AND MUTTON-CHOP SIDEBURNS can all be made from sheepskin. Create a beard from a shallow rectangle of fur, glued along the chin from ear to ear. Twist small strands of fleece into eyebrows and glue in place. Goatees and mustaches can be made from larger twists of fleece.

WISPS AND BABY CURLS are made from clippings of fur or wig hair. Squeeze a nickel-sized blob of FABRITAC glue onto the doll head. Grasp a small bundle of hair and cut it from the hide or fabric backing. Place the blunt-cut end into the glue and hold in place until the glue sets. Continue to glue small clumps of hair in place to form the desired style.

RECYCLED RINGLETS, FALLS, AND FLIPS are easy to fashion out of old wigs. Search the thrift stores for a well-made wig with a foundation at the crown and rows of woof-secured hairs along the back. Carefully cut away the semicircular lace crown, trim to size, and cut out a few notches along the edge. Glue the notches to shape and glue the wig in place.

The back section of the wig can also be reassembled into a variety of hairdos. Experiment with individual woof-strands of hair or cut and shape sections of the wig that are attached to the lining of reinforcement tape. Trim the hair to create the desired style, but be careful—a bad haircut won't grow back!

MOHAIR MANES AND MARCEL CURLS are styled from lengths of mohair attached to a continuous woof-thread. Use this doll wig mohair to create natural-looking hairdos. Buy or make a small pate, or beanie, to fit the doll's head. Attach bands of hair around the pate, starting at the hairline and working up. Cut a small hole in the top of the pate and secure a roll of hair in the opening. Mohair can be combed, curled, cut, and dyed.

PURCHASED PAGE BOYS AND POMPADOURS are just the ticket for your most elaborate dolls. Doll wigs come in a wide variety of sizes, colors, and styles and are readily available at craft stores and doll supply shops.

The four children and their storybook friends are all Fancy Dolls customized to express their individual personalities. All but the seated child and tiny angel are sewn with center front and back seams that add roundness to the heads and torsos. The patterns of the old woodsman and the little boy are further shaped to create protruding noses and tiny chins. The fairy godmother arms are posed with the aid of interior wires that run from her shoulder joints to her needle-sculpted fingertips.

Doll stands can be cleverly disguised as toys or accessories. The woodsman, sewn with rigid hips and flexible arms, stands in place by wrapping an arm around the tree trunk and tucking his hand into the crotch of the tree. The young boy's hoop and blond girl's rocking horse serve as anchors for their small owners. The long, full skirt of the fairy godmother covers a traditional waist-clip stand. The tiny guardian angel, propped without a doll stand, is stuffed with two layers of quilt batting to maintain his flat shape.

BASIC WARDROBE PATTERNS

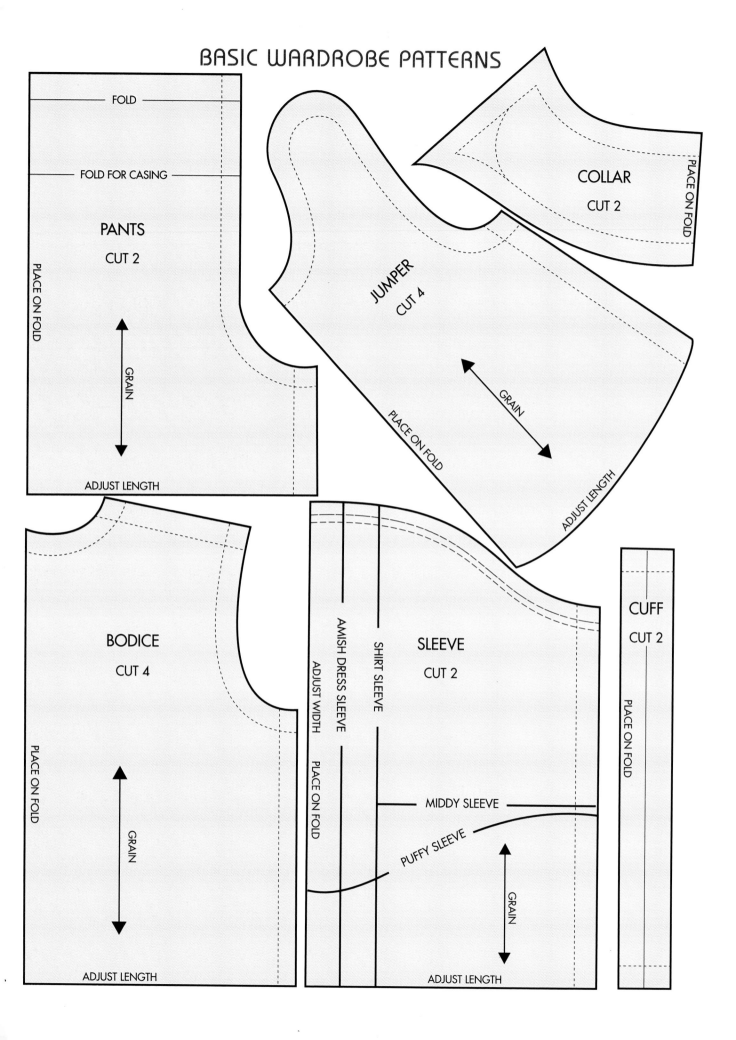

FOLD

FOLD FOR CASING

PANTS
CUT 2

PLACE ON FOLD

GRAIN

ADJUST LENGTH

COLLAR
CUT 2

PLACE ON FOLD

JUMPER
CUT 4

PLACE ON FOLD

GRAIN

ADJUST LENGTH

BODICE
CUT 4

PLACE ON FOLD

GRAIN

ADJUST LENGTH

SLEEVE
CUT 2

ADJUST WIDTH

AMISH DRESS SLEEVE

SHIRT SLEEVE

PLACE ON FOLD

MIDDY SLEEVE

PUFFY SLEEVE

GRAIN

ADJUST LENGTH

CUFF
CUT 2

PLACE ON FOLD

SEWING THE BASIC WARDROBE

Adjust the patterns to fit each doll. If you are a sewing novice, use easy-to-handle cottons such as calico, muslin, percale, and chintz. Quilting cottons are readily available and come in a glorious array of colors and patterns.

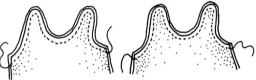

PANTS

Long, short, wide, narrow, straight, or gathered—these pants can be made as outerwear or underwear.

SEW front seam, right sides facing. Clip the curve and press.

SEW a ½" waist casing. Insert elastic and secure at each end.

TURN and hem legs. For bloomers, sew leg casings, thread elastic, and secure at each end.

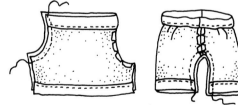

SEW back seam; clip curve; press.

SEW crotch seam. Trim with front bib, straps, or belt loops.

JUMPER

This reversible garment can also be a slip, apron, or blouse. Combine with a gathered skirt to make a dress, or add bloomers for a romper suit.

SEW top edges of jumper, front and back, to linings, right sides facing. Clip curves, turn, and press.

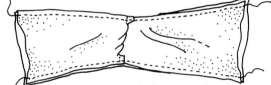

SEW side seam of dress and side seam of lining in one continuous line, right sides facing. Sew other side. Press and fold lining in place.

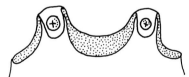

HEM dress and lining to the same length and attach shoulder snaps or buttons.

SHIRT

Adjust this pattern to make dresses, pj's, and coats, as well as shirts and blouses.

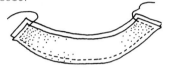

SEW collar to collar lining, right sides facing. Clip curve; turn; press.

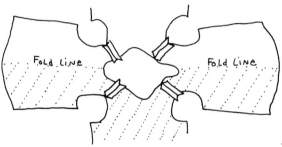

SEW the shoulder seams of shirt bodice fronts and back to bodice linings, right sides facing.

SEW neckline. Baste collar to right side of neckline. Place lining over bodice, matching shoulder seams, right sides facing. Sew neckline, clip curve, turn right side out, and press.

BASTE armholes of bodice to lining.

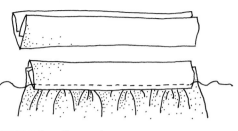

ATTACH cuffs to sleeves. Adjust cuff to fit over the doll's hand. Pleat or gather sleeve edge and bind with double-fold cuff. Press.

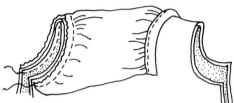

SEW sleeves to bodice/lining. Sew gathering stitches along top of sleeve, adjust to fit armhole. Sew in place, right sides facing.

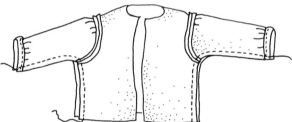

SEW side seams from sleeve cuff to shirttail, right sides facing. Press.

HEM the shirttail or pink the edge if a hem will be too bulky for the tiny garment.

ADD a few details. Sew on snaps or buttons. Create a pocket or add topstitching. Sew a button placket by adding an edging of double-fold binding along one of the front openings.

DRESS

Fashion the jumper into a dress by altering the neckline and sewing shoulder seams and a back or front opening. Add sleeves, a collar, or a sash.

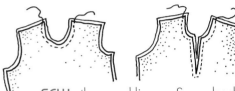

SEW the necklines. Sew bodice front to lining, right sides facing. Sew bodice back to lining, forming a keyhole opening at center back. Clip curves, turn, and press.

SEW shoulder seams of dress and lining, right sides facing. Fold in place and press.

ATTACH the cuffs to the sleeves or sew a casing and thread with elastic.

ATTACH sleeves to bodice. Sew gathering stitches along sleeve tops, adjust, and sew, right sides facing.

SEW side seams from cuffs to hem. Turn, press, and hem dress.

ADD a button and loop at neck opening.

GOWN

Create a queen's ball gown, a baby's christening dress, or an ethnic costume from a combination of shirt and jumper pieces.

TAILOR a fitted bodice from the shirt or jumper pattern by adding front and back darts. Scoop or smock the neckline, or add a full collar.

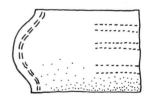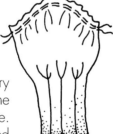

CUSTOMIZE the sleeves. Cut a very wide sleeve and sew tucks along the forearm for a leg-o'-mutton sleeve. Add shoulder ruffles or create fitted sleeves for a colonial look.

SEW a full skirt from a rectangle of fabric. Trim with gathered lace or flounces and combine with layers of starched petticoats. Add panniers, softly gathered at either side of the waist, or a small corset laced with gold braid.

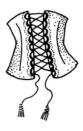

ON YOUR OWN

You are now well on your way to becoming a dollmaker. Continue to investigate new materials, explore new processes, and experiment with new designs. Expand your stash of dollmaking supplies with treasures from thrift stores and yard sales. Most of all, keep making dolls! With every doll that you create, your knowledge and skills will increase and your confidence will grow. Let each doll you complete guide you to the starting point of your next creation.

FOUR • DOLLS OF A NEW DIMENSION

INTERMEDIATE PROJECTS OF CLOTH DOLLS
WITH SCULPTED MODELING PASTE FACES

Modeling paste features, along with special embellishments, add a professional dimension to your dolls. The three big elves on the left have fur wigs, and their painted shoes are trimmed with ribbon and embroidery floss. The features of the dolls on the right are enhanced with an additional layer of embellishment. On the intricately sculpted jester and little boy a base coat of brown paint and a coating of crackle medium are added before their skin tones are applied. The elf has simpler features and a stain buffed finish.

Color Lesson Four: Red and green are **complementary colors.** Located opposite each other on the color wheel, they complete the primary palette of red, yellow, and blue (yellow + blue = green). When red and green are used together, each will make the other appear brighter than when they are used alone or with a noncomplementary color. All opposites on the color wheel, whether red and green, yellow and violet, or orange and blue, are complementary colors and enhance each other when used side by side.

ou will add a new depth to your dollmaking skills when you craft dolls that combine unique cloth bodies with expressive modeling paste faces.

This intermediate project begins with the familiar methods of designing, sewing, and gessoing customized cloth doll bodies and adds the unique process of applying three-dimensional facial features onto the cloth doll heads. The chapter concludes with a discussion about doll stands and includes patterns and instructions for a variety of wardrobe accessories. You can create award-winning shelf sitters with these clear directions.

- Sew a variety of **customized doll bodies.**

- Sculpt **modeling paste facial features,** then gesso, sand, paint, and seal the features. Add wonderful coiffures using the directions in Chapter Three.

- Pose the dolls with **doll stands** that you have cleverly disguised as accessories.

- Create unique costumes by combining the basic clothing in Chapter Three with **wardrobe accessories** of collars, vests, and corsets.

This is an opportunity to practice your basic dollmaking skills while mastering a new and challenging technique. You will be amazed at the professional quality of these beautiful display dolls.

ABOUT SCULPTED DOLLS

Do you remember playing with your favorite doll? Perhaps it was a cloth and composition doll with sleepy eyes that opened and shut, a voice box that bleated "Mama" when the doll was put down, and legs that clattered and clicked when they bumped against one another. These molded dolls with their realistic, sculptured faces, dainty hands and feet, and soft cloth bodies have a long history dating back to ancient times. Early Egyptians and Romans created lifelike burial figures of wood and linen with realistic faces, hands, and feet sculpted of wax. Sculpting materials have always been used to create lifelike, three-dimensional figures for magical and religious rites and, of course, for toys.

By the seventeenth century, Europe's well-developed dollmaking industry produced elegant, natural-looking dolls using combinations of bisque or overglazed porcelain and carved wood, cloth, or kid leather. These exquisite figures were most often the possessions of ladies of royalty and wealth. In the eighteenth century, fragile China dolls were also used as dressmakers' mannequins. Miniature versions of the latest Paris fashions, fitted on shapely little dolls, were displayed far and wide, bringing haute couture to even the most remote town and village. Casting about for ways to make realistic china-like dolls that were affordable to everyone, eighteenth- and nineteenth-century dollmakers tried all kinds of molding compositions. Glues, resins, and sizings were mixed with wood pulp, sawdust, paper pulp, ground bone, shredded rags, linen, wool fiber, egg shells, and flour—just about anything that was pliable, readily available, and cheap. Realistic, molded dolls, once the playthings of rich women, would soon be toys that every child could enjoy.

At first, the best material proved to be a kind of papier-mâché. Later, a wood-pulp substance was used. Your first doll may have been made of one of these materials. Or if you are a little younger, your doll was probably molded of plastic, which became the mainstay of the dollmaking industry by the mid-twentieth century and remains so to this day.

Now you can make beautiful dolls with modeled, lifelike faces. This chapter teaches you how to apply sculpted, three-dimensional features over a firmly stuffed cloth doll body. You will create marvelous, one-of-a-kind display dolls as you add a new dimension to your dollmaking skills.

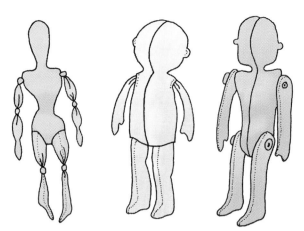

PLANNING AND PREPARING THE DOLL BODY

This doll project will take some time and patience. Plan your work in small stages and be sure to allow for the required drying time between sessions. You may want to work on five or six dolls at a time. Not only does this give you lots of practice with the modeling technique, but it also allows you to rotate your work—as some dolls are drying, others are available for sculpting.

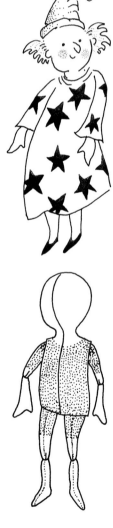

PLAN EACH DOLL before you sew the body. Because the fragile nature of the sculpted features makes these dolls best suited for display rather than vigorous play, you have few practical restrictions in your designs and embellishment. Draw a variety of imaginative dolls in your journal. You might want to create a group of dolls that relate to each other, such as the cast of a favorite story, or replicas of your family members. Make your drawings as detailed as possible. Incorporate a variety of customized features in each doll design and use a touch of needle sculpting to shape the body and form fingers and toes. You could even design your own original doll body pattern! Whichever pattern you begin with, the result will be an unlimited variety of beautifully crafted doll characters and a wonderful sense of accomplishment.

SEW AND STUFF THE DOLL BODIES. Create doll bodies that are as close to your sketches as possible. Use a white or off-white fabric for all areas that are to be covered with modeling paste and gesso. It is easiest to sew the entire doll from the same fabric, but you can create the underwear from printed fabrics that are pieced with, or overlaid on, the basic white fabric. Stuff the dolls very firmly to prevent the sculpted features from cracking. If your doll will be posed in a standing position, omit the hip and knee joints and stuff the torso and legs as one unit.

GESSO the head, arms, and legs of each doll. Apply an even coat of gesso over all the skin tone areas, just as you did for the Fancy Dolls on page 55. Use one coat for the head, and one or more for the arms and legs, depending on how hard you want the finished limbs to be. Sand the dried gesso on the arms and legs, and wipe off all the chalky dust with a damp rag. **Do not sand the gesso that covers the head.** The rough tooth of the unsanded surface will help to hold the paste features in place.

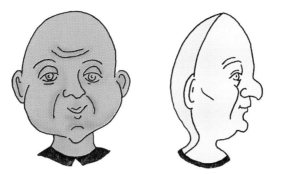

SCULPTING THE FACIAL FEATURES

Now comes the challenging part of this project! You may want to encase the doll bodies in plastic bags, with only their heads and necks exposed. This will keep them clean even if things get a bit messy from the modeling paste. Keep your detailed sketches close at hand. If you are creating the likeness of a particular person, use a photograph or two for reference. Add a few guidelines by lightly penciling the position of the eyes, nose, and mouth. These lines will be covered with paste, gesso, paint, and varnish and will not end up as graphite smears on the doll body.

MODELING PASTE SCULPTING SUPPLIES

Firm doll bodies	Sculpting tools	Clean, lint-free rag
Modeling paste	Gesso	Sandpaper
Bowl of water	Flat paintbrush	Clear varnish

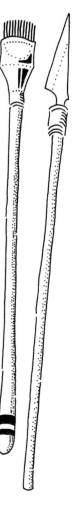

SCULPTING TOOLS

A PARING KNIFE is useful for cutting off pieces of paste from the large block and for smoothing and shaping the features. Rake a serrated blade through the wet paste to create a textured hairdo.

TOOTHPICKS or wooden skewers can be used for incising wrinkle lines, smoothing areas of paste, and poking nostril holes.

A TEASPOON makes a great crimping tool. Use the tip of it to smooth the edges of the paste features onto the fabric head.

PURCHASED CLAY TOOLS such as curved-handle scrapers, metal loops on long handles, and ear-shaped smoothing tools are useful additions to your supply kit.

DENTAL TOOLS make wonderful sculpting implements. Look for picks, scrapers, and curved burnishers at swap meets and medical supply stores.

SCULPTING STEPS

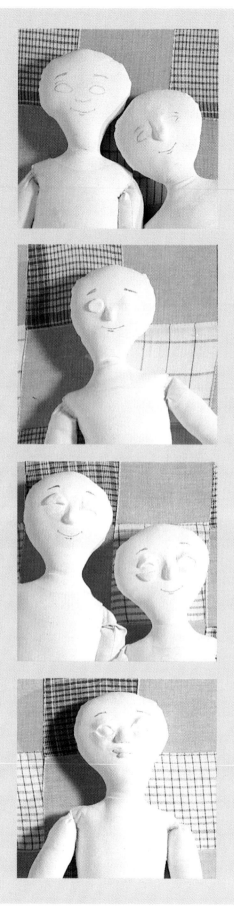

SCULPT THE NOSE. Roll a small cylinder of paste the length of the nose; moisten and press it in place on the face. Smooth, pinch, and pat it into shape. Smooth the surface with your fingertips. Keep your fingertips damp by dipping them as often as necessary into the water bowl. They should be just wet enough to create a slippery film on the surface of the paste, but not so wet as to dilute it and make it runny. This initial step will take some practice. If you create a soggy mess, simply wipe the paste off and try again. It won't be long before you get a feel for the exact amount of moisture needed to build and bond the features.

FORM THE EYES. Roll two balls of paste, flatten them, and press them onto the face. Wet the tip of a spoon or a burnishing tool, and use it to crimp around the edges of each eye to secure it in place. Smooth and taper the surface with your fingertips to create two small mounds.

SHAPE HALF-CIRCLE EYELIDS and attach them to the top of each eye. Crimp along the top edges and taper them to blend into the forehead.

SHAPE THE LOWER LIDS and attach them in the same manner as the upper lids. Smooth and taper the lower edge of each lid into the cheek area.

SHAPE THE LIPS. Roll two small cylinders of paste, press them in place, and crimp along the edges to firmly secure them to the head. Create a bow at the center of the top lip by pushing the paste up and out in a smooth motion. Add small amounts of paste to further shape the lips. Add a layer of paste between the nose and the upper lip and create a small, centered groove from nose to the top of the lips.

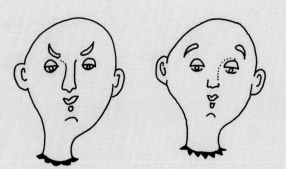

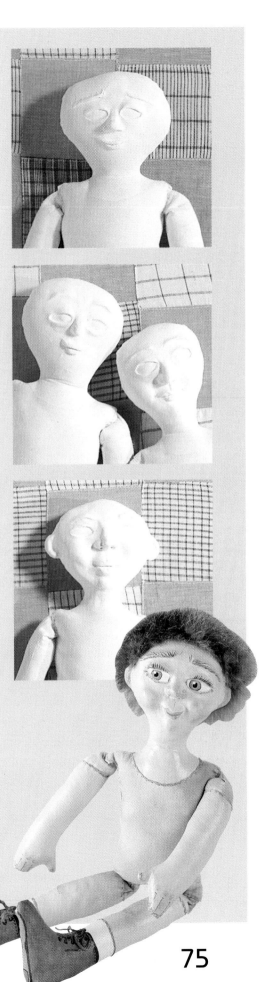

SCULPT THE EYEBROWS. Look at the eyebrow designs in your journal. Notice how their curve and placement affect the facial expression. Close-knit brows suggest a fierce or angry look while high, wide-set brows give a look of surprise.

Roll two cylinders of paste and attach them above the upper eyelids, fitting their shape, size, and placement to the doll character you are sculpting. Shape and smooth each brow.

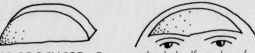

BUILD THE FOREHEAD. Form a thick half-circle of paste the size of the forehead. Dampen and press it in place. Smooth the edges to blend into the surrounding areas. Draw wrinkles with a stylus or toothpick.

ADD CHEEKS AND A CHIN. Roll balls of paste for the cheeks and chin. Slightly flatten each ball, moisten, and secure in place. Blend the edges of the cheeks and chin into the surrounding face.

MODEL THE EARS from thick half-circles of paste and attach them along the side seams. Smooth the base of each ear into the surrounding area.

SMOOTH THE ENTIRE FACE AND AIR DRY THE DOLL. Set it aside for 24 hours, allowing the paste to dry slowly and naturally. Heat from a hair dryer may cause the paste to shrink unevenly and crack as it dries. If cracks should appear once the paste is dry, fill them with softened modeling paste and smooth the patches with wet fingertips.

CONTINUE TO BUILD THE FACE, adding additional layers of paste ¼" at a time. Smooth each layer with your wet fingertips and let it air dry slowly and naturally.

75

Here are dolls in various stages of embellishment starting with the gessoed doll body in the upper left corner. Unpainted areas become the dolls' chemises and are trimmed with embroidery. The underwear of the two dolls in the lower right corner is tea stained for a touch of soft color. Thin washes of dye can also be used to add color without stiffening the fabric.

DECORATING AND DRESSING THE DOLL

When the final layers of modeling paste are thoroughly dry, decorate and dress each doll. Refer to your journal sketches as you paint the faces and sew the costumes. If a doll's features did not turn out exactly as you had planned, redraw the face design and the clothing to fit the character that you have created.

SAND THE FEATURES. If you should accidentally chip a section or sand away more than you had planned, moisten and patch the area with additional paste, dry for 24 hours, and sand it again.

GESSO THE ENTIRE HEAD of each doll. Apply one coat of gesso and let it air dry overnight. Add and dry a few more coats to smooth out the features. Gently sand the gessoed head.

PAINT AND SEAL THE DOLLS following the instructions for Fancy Dolls on pages 55–57. For a naturalistic look, blend the blush into the skin tones.

Because acrylic paint dries quickly, it is usually applied wet-on-dry, making it difficult to blend. Many dollmakers prefer to use slow-drying oil paint, which allows them to work wet-on-wet, creating a more lifelike blending of color. Oil paint must be thinned and cleaned with turpentine. **Never** mix water-base acrylics with traditional oil-base products. There is, however, a water-soluble oil paint which combines oil's blendability with acrylic's ease of cleanup. Try all three paints to find your favorite.

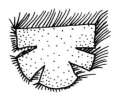

CREATE A WIG from fur, or recycle a wig using the directions on pages 58–59. Glue the wig in place after you have sealed the paint with varnish.

DRESS EACH DOLL in an imaginative outfit created from Chapter Three's wardrobe patterns, creating a collar, vest, or corset for added embellishment. Pose the finished doll with the aid of a stand that has been cleverly disguised as an accessory. A discussion of doll stands and instructions for wardrobe accessories conclude this chapter.

YOUR DOLLS ARE NOW COMPLETE. Whether they stand or sit or dance, enjoy each for what it is—a beautiful new addition to your doll collection and the expressive result of your growing dollmaking skills.

The basic wardrobe patterns and accessories are customized to make each of these unique elf costumes. Nubbly wool, deep pile velvet, soft dimity, and polished chintz add textural interest to the tiny clothes. Old cotton hankies are fashioned into the blouse and skirt of the redheaded doll. The gathered skirts and petticoats are sewn from rectangles of fabric. Attach the petticoat to the hem of the blouse to reduce the amount of bulk at the waist.

It is a challenge to create a soft drape of the fabric in tiny doll clothes. Even the thinnest of fabrics can appear unnaturally stiff. Avoid bulky, double-folded hems and use soft, light-weight fabric for facings and casings. Substitute look-alike materials when possible. Velour has the sheen and nap of velvet but is less bulky when gathered into tiny waist bands; light-weight flannel has the look of wool without the added thickness. Old, worn fabrics drape in a more realistic manner than newer ones.

DOLL STANDS

Display dolls, like shelf standees and bed sitters, are often posed with the aid of a doll stand. Many commercial stands are available. Some stands hold the doll in position with a semicircular waist clip; others have a saddle-shaped seat for the doll to straddle. A narrow dowel attached to a base makes an inconspicuous stand. The post can be threaded under trouser legs or skirts and the doll attached with heavy thread. Whichever type of stand you use, select a size that allows the doll to balance properly.

I prefer to create original stands that become a part of the doll's accessories. This makes the doll more lively and the stand less conspicuous. It also adds a decorative element to the display. If the doll was designed to sit, sew the arms to the top of the legs with a few hidden stitches to keep the doll in position. You can also attach the doll to a small chair, miniature hay bale, or other object like a bicycle or wagon. For standing poses, combine a doll with rigid legs and no hip or knee joints with an interesting accessory like a broom, cane, or small tree to form a tripod, the most stable balance there is.

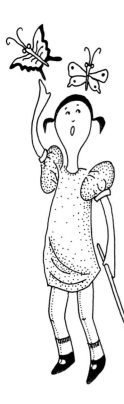

Plan the stand as you plan the doll. Sketch a few designs in your journal. Decide how you want to position the doll. Will it stand or sit? What gesture will the arms make? Will the doll be holding a prop? How will the feet be positioned? Design both the doll and stand to accommodate the pose. Wire the arms if they are to be posed, and be sure to firmly stuff the legs for standing characters. Choose a prop that will complement the doll. A woodsman might be balanced with a small tree, a few logs, or an ax. A child could be holding a jump rope that has been re-enforced with stabilizing wire, or leaning on building blocks or a scooter with high handlebars.

Enjoy the challenge of designing attractive stands that are tailor-made for each of your display dolls. Remember, the less the stand looks like a stand, the more animated your dolls will appear.

WARDROBE ACCESSORY PATTERNS

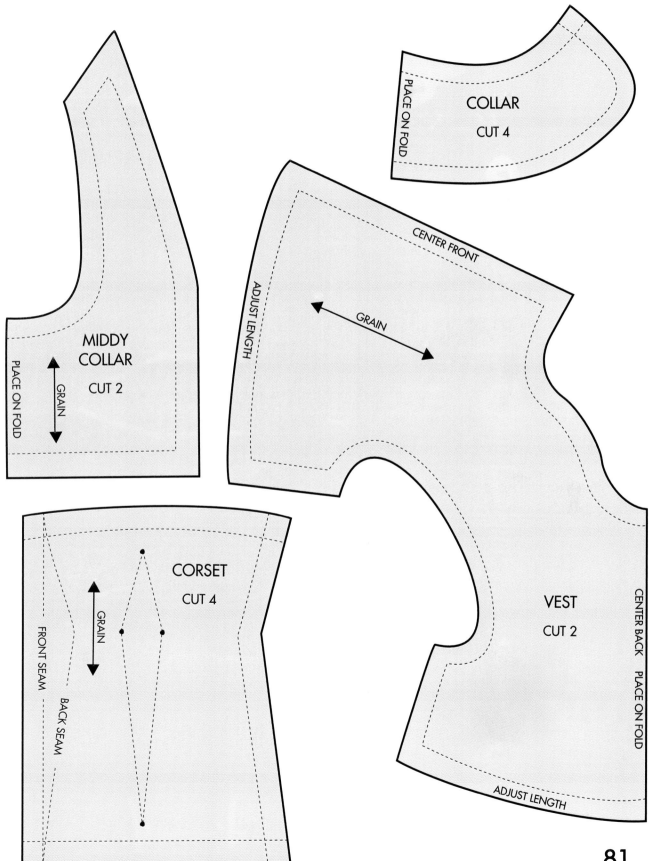

PLACE ON FOLD

COLLAR

CUT 4

MIDDY COLLAR

CUT 2

PLACE ON FOLD

GRAIN

CENTER FRONT

ADJUST LENGTH

GRAIN

VEST

CUT 2

CENTER BACK   PLACE ON FOLD

ADJUST LENGTH

CORSET

CUT 4

GRAIN

FRONT SEAM

BACK SEAM

81

SEWING THE WARDROBE ACCESSORIES

All the accessories are designed to intermix with the basic wardrobe on pages 62–65. You may have to adjust them to fit your customized dolls. Sew them from unusual combinations of fabrics and notions.

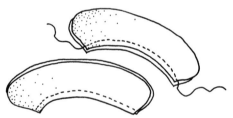

REMOVABLE COLLAR

Extend the versatility of the basic clothing with wide bertha collars, rounded Peter Pans, and pointed shirt collars. Adjust the pattern to fit each doll's neck. Cut four.

SEW the neckline of two collars together, right sides facing, clip curves, open out, and press. Repeat.

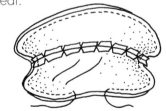

PIN and sew the two sewn pairs together, right sides facing. Leave a small opening for turning. Clip curves, turn, close the opening, and press.

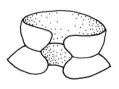

TRIM with a button and loop, a perky little bow, or a silk flower.

MIDDY COLLAR

Sew the middy collar onto front-opening garments, or create a removable collar for garments that open in the back. Cut two.

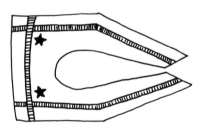

DECORATE the right side of one collar with braid, leaving a seam allowance around the edges.

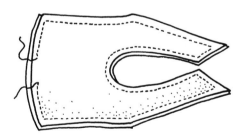

SEW the collars together, right sides facing, leaving a small opening for turning. Clip curves, turn, close opening, and press. Add a necktie or a big floppy bow.

VEST

This reversible jerkin is perfect for male and female costumes. Sew a button-front vest by adding extra width to the front sections. Cut one vest and one lining.

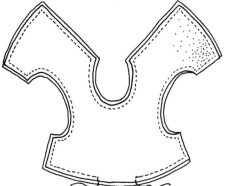

SEW vest to lining, right sides facing, leaving a small opening at the center back for turning. Clip curves, turn, sew closed, and press.

OVERLAP side seams to fit, and sew by hand or machine.

TRIM with hand or machine topstitching, or add braid, binding, buttons, or bows.

CORSET

Cinch the tiny waist of a princess, milkmaid, dowager, or diva with this dainty outer- or undergarment. Sew the corset from muslin to check the fit. Cut two backs and four fronts.

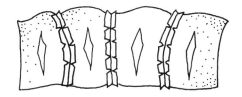

SEW darts and side seams of the corset, right sides facing. Repeat for lining. Trim darts and press.

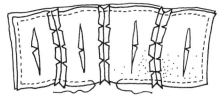

SEW corset to lining, right sides facing. Leave a small opening for turning. Clip curves, turn, close opening, and press.

ADD trims and loops for lacing. Thread with gold braid or satin rattail. Decorate underwear with machine topstitching in a contrasting color, or add garters trimmed with ribbon.

ON YOUR OWN

So much of dollmaking expertise comes from the little discoveries, shortcuts, and inventions that you develop as you make doll after doll. Tools and materials that once seemed to have a mind of their own become familiar and easy-to-manage, and techniques that were difficult to master become the means of self-expression—you'll even find yourself adding your own special crafting nuances. And somewhere along the way, quite unexpectedly, you will be transformed from someone who makes dolls into a dollmaker.

FIVE • MEDLEY DOLLS

ADVANCED DOLL PROJECTS
THAT COMBINE CLOTH DOLL BODIES WITH
POLYMER CLAY HEADS, HANDS, AND FEET

The personality of each Medley Doll begins with the selection of polymer clay. The old man's rich brown skin is blended from a small amount of brown Fimo and a larger quantity of white Sculpey. The pale pink child is sculpted from a mixture of white Sculpey, translucent PROMAT, and pink Super Sculpey. Super Sculpey creates the red-headed girl's ruddy complexion, while Cernit is the clay used for her long-haired friend. The little pink child and the long-haired girl have rooted hair, embedded while the clay was pliable.

Color Lesson Five: Carefully **balance** the color selection and arrangement of each doll project using a practical combination I call **most, less, and least.** Choose three main colors for each outfit. Designate one color as the **dominant hue** *(most)*, one as the **secondary color** *(less)*, and the third as the **accent** *(least)*. By limiting the number of colors and carefully controlling the amount of each, you can achieve a pleasing unity in all your color arrangements.

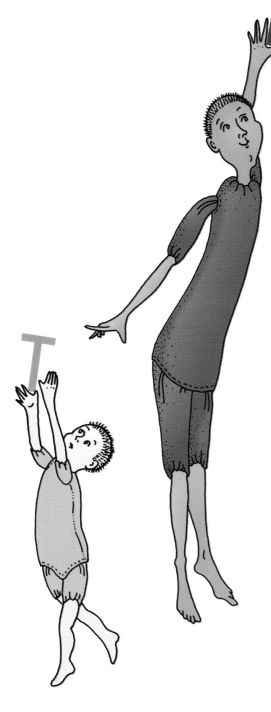

Turn a medley of materials into prizewinning creations. This advanced dollmaking project combines finely detailed heads, hands, and feet of polymer clay with jointed cloth bodies. Dress each doll in a most imaginative outfit. The results are amazing!

This chapter presents all the information needed to make beautiful creations and includes patterns and directions for hats, fairy wings, and shoes. You can accessorize your wonderful dolls from head to toe!

- Sculpt **polymer clay doll heads** with expressive features and **lifelike hands and feet.**

- Add rooted **hairdos** before baking the head, or glue on wigs after baking.

- Create **cloth bodies** with adjustable casings at neck, wrist, and ankle. Attach the baked clay pieces to the stuffed doll bodies.

- Sew splendid outfits with **finishing touches** that include hats, shoes, and even wings.

These dolls take a little time and practice, but the work is worth the wonderful results. You'll treasure these exquisite, heirloom creations for years to come.

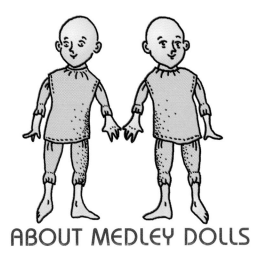

ABOUT MEDLEY DOLLS

Clays have been used to sculpt doll-like figures since prehistoric times. Red terra-cotta, dug from the earth and mixed with coarse sand, was used to form the oldest known sculptures—buxom fertility goddesses. Ever since, a multitude of clays, each with its unique color and texture, has paraded through the long history of dollmaking.

An entirely new sculpting material, discovered in a laboratory rather than dug from the earth, was developed in the 1930s by German chemists. Credit is given to Sophie Rehbinder-Kruse, the daughter of the famous dollmaker Käthe Kruse. Ms. Rehbinder-Kruse was also a dollmaker and needed a composition for the commercial production of dolls that was easy to mold, lifelike in color and translucency, and inexpensive to manufacture. The result was the creation of polymer modeling compound from which Ms. Rehbinder-Kruse sculpted dozens of life-sized mannequins. It did not prove a suitable material for factory-produced dolls, but it has become increasingly popular as a material for the professional artisan, jewelrymaker, home crafter, and dollmaker.

Polymer clay is an ideal material for sculpting the heads, hands, and feet of the Medley Doll. It is very pliable, bakes at a low temperature in your oven, and comes in a variety of skin colors. You can imbed hair into the unbaked head and glass eyes into the eye sockets. Attach the baked clay pieces to an easy-to-make cloth doll body with drawstring casings at the neck, wrists, and ankles and voilá—you have a delightful doll!

Before you begin, be sure to read about polymer clay on pages 36–37. Select the brand of clay you will use. If you have never worked with a polymer modeling compound, I recommend that you use Sculpey or Super Sculpey for your first efforts. Next, experiment with Fimo. When you feel confident in your handling of the clay, use Cernit for your more advanced projects.

Some dollmakers find it easiest to make the body, then sculpt the head, hands, and feet to fit. Others make the polymer pieces first, then adjust the size of the body. I suggest that you make a doll with each method and decide for yourself which works best for you.

PLANNING THE DOLL DESIGN

If you have never worked with polymer clay you might find it easiest to make character dolls rather that beautiful ones. It is much more difficult to model a beautiful face than to create a face with unusual features like that of an old person, gnome, witch, hag, sorceress, or elf. Character dolls offer a lot more creative freedom when it comes to shaping the features.

Determine the age, sex, occupation, and size of your dolls. Draw a number of ideas in your journal. Plan the joint design. You may want to review the material on customizing the doll body on pages 13–19. The fragility of the polymer clay makes these dolls well suited for display, so pose your dolls in animated gestures and incorporate doll stands as interesting accessories.

Select the fabric and stuffing that you will use. The polymer heads tend to make the dolls slightly top-heavy, so you might want to balance the dolls by filling the lower part of the bodies with heavy pellets, sand, or buckshot. Be cautious, however, since these fillers tend to spill out of the open casings; it is best to only use them when you are ready to assemble the cloth and clay pieces.

Sketch the hairdos, and select the methods of construction. Hair can be rooted into the unbaked scalp, then styled after the head is baked, or a wig can be glued in place once the polymer sections are hardened.

Design glorious costumes. Browse through the costume books in the theater section of your local library, or leaf through magazines for inspiration. Old copies of the *National Geographic* are a great source for diverse ethnic costumes; fashion magazines provide haute-couture. Combine a symphony of unusual fabrics with sharp accessories. These dolls will surely be something to sing about!

SCULPTING THE HEAD

Keep your journal sketches in front of you as you work. Also, it can help to use two small mirrors to examine your own face, front, and profile as you sculpt the doll's face. Check out the alignment of your head and neck and the shape of your forehead, chin, and nose. Refer to the step-by-step photographs on the following pages as you sculpt the clay pieces.

SCULPTING SUPPLIES

Polymer clay	Wire
Sculpting tools	Wire cutters
Airtight plastic bag	Baking sheet
Aluminum foil	Sculpting armature

SCULPTING ARMATURE

To make an armature, cut a square of wood, 5" x 5" x 1". Drill a ½" hole in the center and fit with an 8" dowel. Secure the dowel in place with wood glue.

SCULPTING TOOLS

The sculpting tools listed on page 73 can also be used to work with polymer clay. In addition, you may find the following items useful.

A ROLLING PIN can be improvised from a piece of 1" dowel. Roll the clay between two risers of the desired height to ensure an even thickness of clay.

AN OVEN THERMOMETER will prevent you from overheating the clay. Keep in mind that the temperature settings on most ovens are not accurate.

A KITCHEN TIMER is a must—the louder the better!

SCULPTING STEPS

CRUMPLE A SHEET OF ALUMINUM FOIL into a tightly packed egg-shaped ball, slightly smaller than your fist. If you are using an armature, smooth a piece of foil over the dowel, and push the foil head onto the top of the dowel, making the dowel the core of the neck. Smooth a final piece of foil over the entire head and neck to secure the head to the armature.

KNEAD SIX OUNCES OF CLAY until it becomes a soft, pliable mass, then roll it into a ¼"-thick pancake.

PLACE THE PANCAKE ON TOP OF THE FOIL HEAD and wrap the entire head and neck with the clay. Smooth the surface of the clay and lightly mark the position of the eyes, nose, and mouth with a toothpick or stylus.

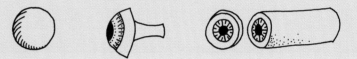

MODEL THE EYEBALLS. Roll two balls of white clay and bake at 275° for 15 minutes. Indent the sockets and press the hardened eyeballs into place. Glass eyes can also be used. Avoid plastic eyes that may melt when baked. If you are a polymer clay artist, create a millefiori cane with an eye design and then slice off eyes, round the edges, and bake as needed.

MAKE THE NOSE. Roll out a small cylinder of clay the length of the nose and press it in place. Roll two beads and press them on either side for nostrils. Smooth and shape. Poke nostril holes with a toothpick or stylus.

CREATE THE LIPS. Press two small cylinders into place and shape with your fingers or a dental pick. Adjust and shape the area between the nose and upper lip.

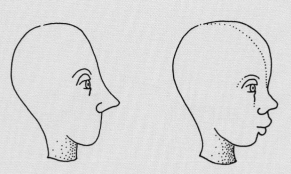

SHAPE THE FOREHEAD AND ADD EYELIDS. Press a cylinder of clay along the browline. Add a half circle of clay above the brow and smooth it into shape. Cut out small half-circles for the upper eyelids and press them into place atop the eyeballs. Add lower lids and blend them into the cheeks.

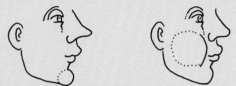

BUILD THE CHIN, CHEEKS, AND EARS. Press a small ball in place to form a chin. Check the profile and adjust the shape. Flatten two balls and smooth onto the cheek areas. Shape thick half circles into ears and press in place.

SMOOTH THE FACE and draw laugh lines and wrinkles with a stylus.

MAKE A NECK CASING GROOVE. Press a channel around the neck, ¼" from the end. Create a small lip around the end of the neck.

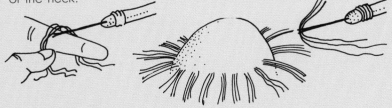

ROOT THE HAIR. Imbed a long needle into a pencil eraser and clip off the top half of the eye. Use this tool to poke tiny clumps of doll hair into the soft scalp. Begin at the hairline and work toward the crown.

SET THE SOFT CLAY HEAD ASIDE while you sculpt the hands and feet since it's best to bake all of the clay pieces at the same time to ensure even color and density.

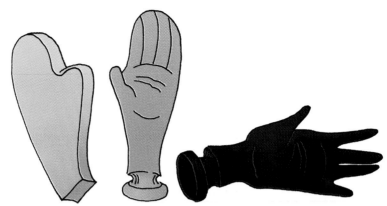

SCULPTING THE HANDS AND ARMS

Mitten-shaped hands are easy-to-make and can be shaped to hold accessories. Draw and cut out a paper template of the flat mitten shaped hand with an arm of the desired length.

SCULPT THE HAND AND ARM. Roll out a large ½"-thick pancake of clay. Press the template lightly into the clay to mark the two hands. Cut out the clay pieces and round off the edges. Add more clay if necessary and create round arms and narrow wrists. Bend the mitten fingers into a grasp and adjust the thumb. Incise lines to indicate individual fingers and nails.

FORM A CASING GROOVE. Press a groove around the arm, ¼" from the end. Shape a lip of clay around the end of the arm.

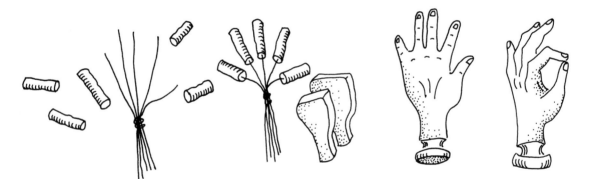

Hands with delineated fingers are reinforced with wire. Cut out five 4"-long wires or pipe cleaners for each hand. Arrange in the shape of a hand and twist together to form fingers, wrist, and arm. Trim excess wire.

ROLL FINGER-SIZE CYLINDERS OF CLAY and thread them onto the finger wires. Encase the palm and arm wire with more clay, and pinch and pat into shape. Bend the hand into the desired position and smooth the entire piece. Draw creases, knuckles, and nails with a toothpick or stylus.

FORM A CASING GROOVE at the end of the arm using the directions given for the mitten-shaped hand. Make sure the clay arm is smaller in circumference than the cloth casing opening.

94

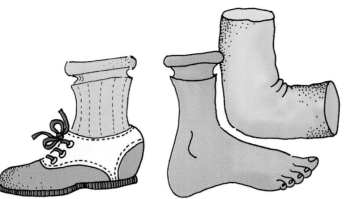

SCULPTING THE FEET AND LEGS

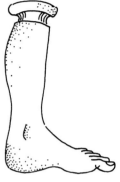

Bare legs and feet can be fitted with shoes sewn from the patterns and directions at the end of this chapter. Individualize the size and shape to fit the age of each doll character you make.

ROLL A CLAY CYLINDER the width of each leg. Bend the cylinders to form the legs and feet. Flatten each foot and pinch and pull to form the arch, heel, and toes. Narrow the ankles and incise lines to mark the toes, joint creases, and nails. Create a casing groove at the top of each leg. You may want to insert reinforcement wires in each piece for added strength.

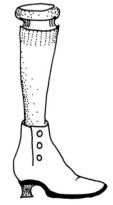

Permanent shoes or boots, reminiscent of those found on old-fashioned china dolls, are created in much the same way as the barefeet. Sculpt with colored clays or paint and varnish the shoes after they are baked.

ROLL A CLAY CYLINDER and bend to form each leg and foot. Flatten the bottom of the foot and shape the toe and the arch. Add a heel and sole, then add some interesting details such as a design of tiny stitches, straps, or buttons. You might even punch shoelace holes into a flap of clay, and thread it with real laces after the piece is fired.

CREATE THE CASING GROOVE at the top of each leg.

HEAT SET THE CLAY PIECES

Gently ease the head off the dowel and fill the hollow core of the neck with clay. Place all the clay pieces on a foil-covered cookie sheet and brace any section that might sag with twists of foil or heatproof glass bowls. Bake the clay pieces for 30 minutes in a preheated 275° oven. Cool before handling. Additional clay may be added to the hardened clay, and the pieces can be rebaked as often as needed.

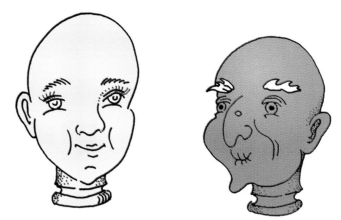

DECORATING THE HEAD, HANDS, AND FEET

Apply facial makeup directly onto the hardened, flesh-tone head. White clay must first be colored with a flesh tone before the makeup is added. An allover coloring with a brush-tip fabric pen gives the skin a luminous tint and can be heat set in the oven. When the piece has cooled, apply the cosmetics you use on your own face and accent with fine-point permanent pens and brush-tip fabric pens. After applying the cosmetics, **bake the head in a 275° oven for fifteen minutes** to permanently bond the color to the clay. The head can also be gessoed and decorated with acrylic paint. Add details with paint and fabric pen and varnish when dry. **Do not bake the acrylic paint.**

DECORATING SUPPLIES

Colored pencils	Water jar	Eye shadow
Paintbrushes	Clean, lint-free rag	Clear varnish
Paints	Cheek blush	Palette

Assorted brush-tip fabric pens and fine-point permanent pens
Optional: Fiber eyelashes, White glue

BLUSH THE CHEEKS, EARS, CHIN, AND MOUTH with a soft brush of rouge, just as you would your own face. Blend the blush into the skin color. Redden the mouth with a blush that is darker than the cheek blush. Make the upper lip a little darker than the lower one.

COLOR THE EYES. Draw the irises and pupils onto white clay eyeballs with fine-point permanent pens. Fill in the color with a brush-tip fabric pen.

SHADE THE EYELIDS with a touch of eye shadow. Blend the color around the outside corners of each eye.

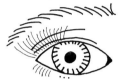

ADD EYEBROWS AND LASHES. Use a fine-point permanent pen to draw the brows and upper and lower lashes, or glue fiber eyelashes along the eyelids and twists of fur along the brow line.

BLUSH THE HEELS, TOES, PALMS, AND FINGERS. Tint the wrinkle lines with a brush-tip fabric pen. Draw the nails with a fine-point permanent pen.

ADD A HAIRDO. Rooted hair, inserted into the doll head when the clay was soft, can be cut, curled, and styled after the head has been baked and the face decorated. If you have not rooted the hair, create a wig of fur or fiber and glue it in place on the hardened head. Use the directions on pages 58–59 to fashion a hairstyle and add twists of fleece for eyebrows, and mustaches. For those extra-fancy hairdos, consider buying a doll wig. Realistic hairdos in a variety of sizes, styles, and colors are available in doll supply shops. Attach them with FABRITAC or white glue.

THE TORSO PATTERN

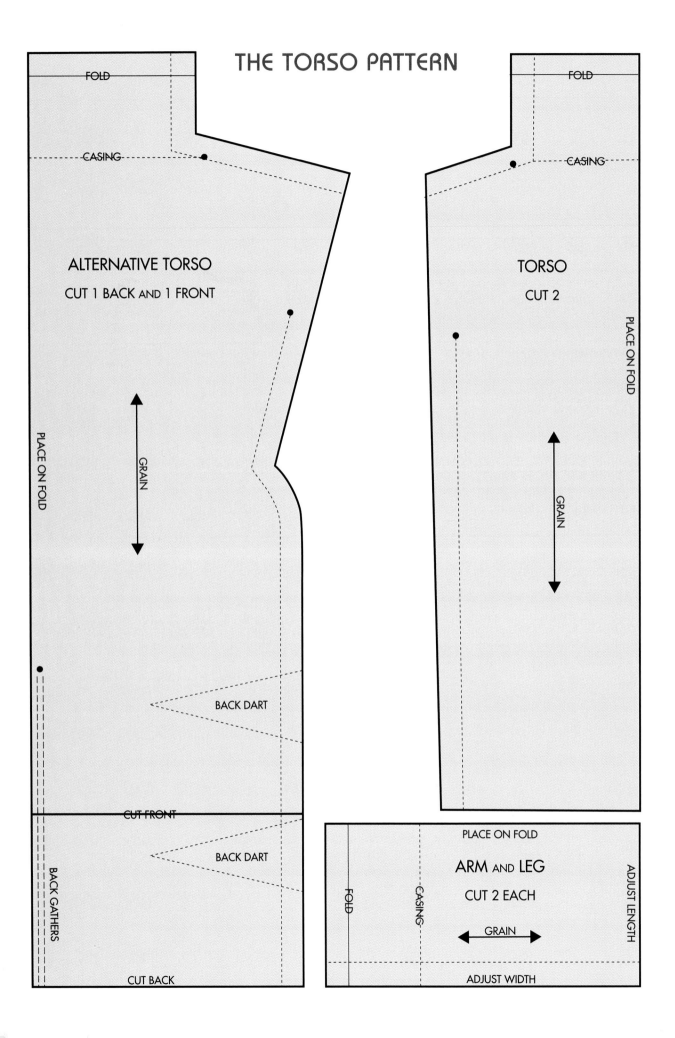

FOLD

FOLD

CASING

CASING

ALTERNATIVE TORSO

CUT 1 BACK AND 1 FRONT

TORSO

CUT 2

PLACE ON FOLD

PLACE ON FOLD

GRAIN

GRAIN

BACK DART

CUT FRONT

BACK DART

BACK GATHERS

CUT BACK

PLACE ON FOLD

ARM AND LEG

CUT 2 EACH

FOLD

CASING

ADJUST LENGTH

GRAIN

ADJUST WIDTH

SEWING THE TORSO

Gather your sewing supplies, fabric, and 1½ yards of narrow ribbon. Adjust the pattern to fit the clay pieces. Cut two bodies, two arms and two legs. Cut the ribbon into five equal pieces. Lengths of 22-gauge florist wire may be substituted for the ribbon.

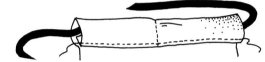

SEW THE ARMS AND LEGS. Sew a casing along one end of each arm and leg. Thread each casing with ribbon and stitch through the center to secure. Fold each arm and each leg lengthwise, right sides facing. Sew from the top to the casing stitches. Turn and press.

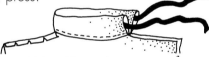

SEW THE BODY SEAMS. Place the torso sections together, right sides facing. Sew one side from the top of the neck to the shoulder and from under the arm to the hem. Clip curves and press the seam open. Sew a neck casing, thread it with ribbon, and stitch through the center of the casing to secure. Sew the remaining seam from the casing stitches to the shoulder and from the underarm to hem. Clip curves, press, and turn right side out. Baste the hem.

ATTACH THE ARMS AND LEGS. Fit the clay pieces into the casing ends and adjust the length of the arms and legs. Mark the positions of the elbows and knees on the cloth before removing the clay pieces. Double-fold the top of the arms and sew two parallel rows of stitches ¼" and ½" from top. Fold an inverted pleat at either side of each leg top and sew two rows of parallel stitches. Insert cloth arms and legs in the torso and topstitch to secure.

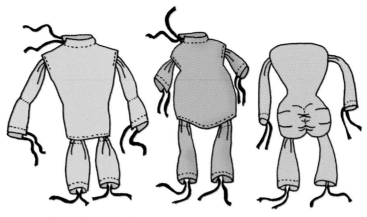

CUSTOMIZING THE TORSO

Adapt the body to suit the design you envision by using the customizing suggestions on pages 13–19. Experiment with various joint constructions, and change the height and girth of the torso to fit your special character. Shorten the fabric arms and legs and lengthen the polymer clay pieces if you want the arms and legs to show on the finished doll.

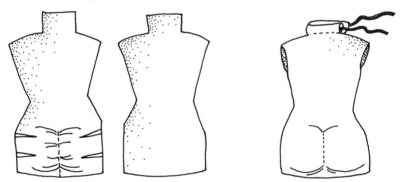

FASHION A SHAPELY DERRIÈRE using the alternative torso pattern. Sew two small darts at either side of the hips and adjust the centered line of gathering stitches to form rounded buttocks. Be sure that the finished length of the adjusted back section matches the length of the front section.

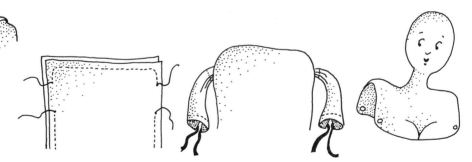

MAKE A DOLL WITH A DARING DÉCOLLETAGE by adding a polymer breastplate to the clay neck. This age-old design was commonly used for china and porcelain dolls. Sew straight across the top of the cloth body from shoulder to shoulder, omitting the neck casing. Sculpt the breastplate to fit over the top of the firmly stuffed cloth body. Before baking, punch small holes along the edge of the plate. Sew it onto the body after it is baked.

COMBINE A POLYMER HEAD WITH CLOTH HANDS AND FEET. Wired cloth fingers allow the doll to hold items and can be easily adjusted into a variety of different poses. Cloth feet, painted with a stocking design, can be fitted with decorative shoes that become part of the doll's stand.

DO NOT SEW THE KNEE AND ELBOW JOINTS until you have stuffed the torso and the upper limbs. Adjust the amount of stuffing in the upper arms and legs according to the doll's final pose. An unstuffed or lightly stuffed arm is flexible and easy-to-pose while a firmly stuffed one will maintain an outstretched gesture. A lightly stuffed thigh is best for a seated doll.

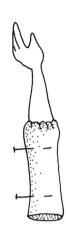

ASSEMBLE THE DOLL

SEW THE ELBOW AND KNEE JOINTS. Stuff the upper arms and legs and form a small inverted pleat on either side of each joint. Sew across the elbow and knee joints before stuffing the lower arms and legs.

STUFF THE TORSO firmly with stuffing or weight it with heavy pellets.

ATTACH THE HEAD. Fit the neck into the casing, then tighten the casing ribbon around the neck groove. Secure it with a tight knot.

ATTACH THE HANDS AND FEET. Fit the clay pieces into the casings, tighten the casing ribbon around the casing grooves, and secure.

GOOD JOB! Your doll is now complete—except for that glorious costume you are now ready to sew and accessorize.

The little shoemakers are bundled up in warm sweaters, hats, and leggings sewn from an array of thrift store clothing. Their playful mix-and-match outfits of diverse floral prints, stripes, plaids, and woolly textures are carefully balanced using the application of *Most, Less, and Least* (page 87). Even the most unexpected and unusual combinations of textures, patterns, and colors can be unified into a pleasing whole when the amount and placement of each is carefully considered.

When sewing knits or other stretchy fabrics be sure to use a universal sewing machine needle or one specially made just for knits. The rounded tip will not snag or tear the delicate threads of the fabric. Stitch all the seams with a zigzag or satin stitch to prevent the seam thread from breaking when the fabric is stretched. To lessen bulky selvage along the seams of heavy wool sweaters, sew the seams with a narrow satin stitch and trim off all excess fabric.

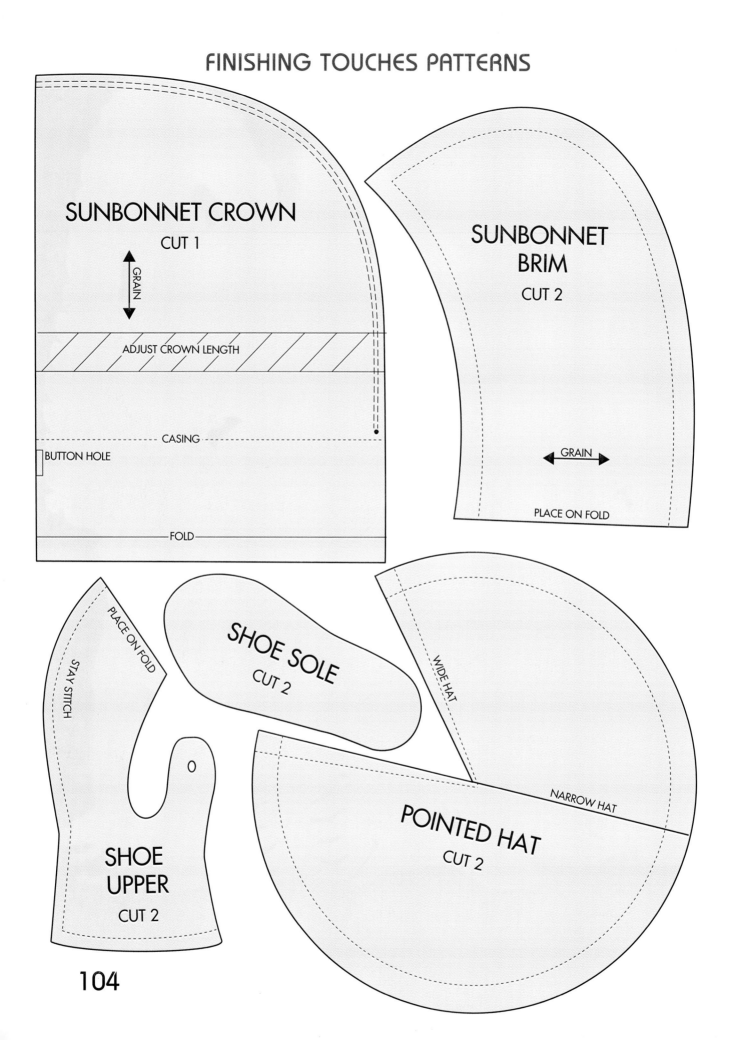

SUNBONNET CROWN

CUT 1

GRAIN

ADJUST CROWN LENGTH

CASING

BUTTON HOLE

FOLD

SUNBONNET
BRIM

CUT 2

GRAIN

PLACE ON FOLD

PLACE ON FOLD

STAY STITCH

SHOE SOLE

CUT 2

WIDE HAT

NARROW HAT

SHOE
UPPER

CUT 2

O

POINTED HAT

CUT 2

SEWING THE FINISHING TOUCHES

reate small-scale accents to complete each of your doll's costumes. Beautifully crafted details add a professional quality to your projects and will elicit oohs and aahs from admirers of your dollmaking skills.

POINTED CAP

Adjust the radius and arc of this cone-shaped pattern to create caps of various heights and widths. Cut one hat and one lining.

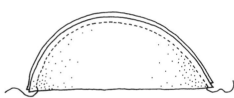

SEW curved brim of hat to lining, right sides facing. Clip curve.

SEW seam. Fold hat, matching brim seam, and sew, leaving an opening along lining. Trim ends, turn, close opening, and fit lining in hat.

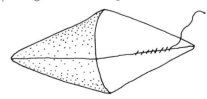

TRIM with a bell, feathers, flowers, or a pom-pom.

SUNBONNET

Sew Amish hats, baby caps, and spring bonnets from this classic design. Cut two brims and one crown.

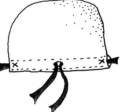

SEW brims, right sides facing. Clip curve, turn, and press.

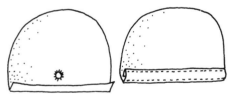

FORM casing at back of crown. Turn and press a ½" casing along flat edge of crown. Work a small buttonhole at top center of casing as marked. Sew the casing. Thread and secure casing ribbons.

SEW crown to brim. Adjust crown's gathering stitches to fit brim. Sew crown to top side of brim, right sides facing. Turn under and hand sew remaining brim edge. Add chin straps.

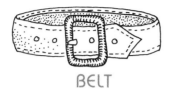

BELT

An old watchband buckle and a thrift store leather sash combine to make this stylish accoutrement.

CUT leather strip ½" longer and wider than the desired size. Turn under and sew ¼" at long edges. Clip to a point at one end.

ATTACH buckle ½" from end and sew across belt to secure. Measure doll's waist and punch small buckle holes to fit.

SUSPENDERS

Use an additional length of the leather sash, four small buttons, and some carpet twine to fashion these tiny braces.

CUT two straps ½" wider and ¾" longer than desired size. Turn under and sew ¼" at long edges.

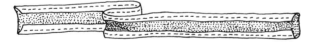

TURN under and sew strap ends. Thread and tie a small loop of twine at each end.

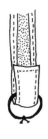

SEW buttons to pants and attach straps by the twine loops.

FLOWER WINGS

Buy two wire-stemmed flowers that complement the doll's costume.

CUT each stem to the width of the doll's back and twist them together.

SEW this wire connector to the doll's back.

WIRED-RIBBON WINGS

Use 2"- or 3"-wide wired ribbon to make these gossamer fairy wings.

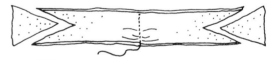

CUT a length of ribbon the width of the wings, gather the center and secure. Sew on doll. Cut a V-shape at ends, and bend to shape.

COMBINE two lengths of ribbon for the double wings of insects and butterflies.

106

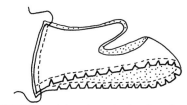

SHOES

Sew these shoes from soft leather or heavy fabric. For fabric shoes, bond a lining fabric to the upper's fabric with fusible webbing. Cut out two fabric or leather uppers, two thin cardboard inner soles, two sole fillers from the upper's fabric, and two heavy cardboard outer soles. Use hinged clothespins to clamp the glued pieces. After you have mastered this basic doll shoe, try your hand at fancy boots, slippers, and lace-up oxfords.

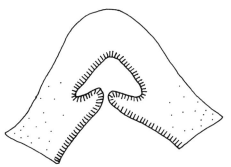

BIND the top edge of the uppers with a tight buttonhole stitch or machine-sewn satin stitch.

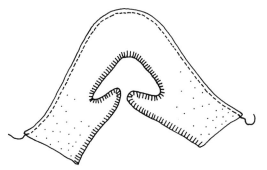

SEW a line of staystitches ⅛" from the uppers' bottom edge.

SEW and backstitch the back seam from top to staystitches. Notch the upper's bottom edge below the staystitch line.

GLUE the upper to the inner sole at the center front and back, and clamp with clothespins. Glue and clamp the remaining edges and stuff with tissue until dry. Or you may prefer to handstitch the upper to the inner sole.

TRIM the filler to fit, and glue in place. Glue on the outer sole, and clamp till dry.

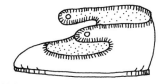

MAKE holes for ribbon ties with a paper punch and bind with buttonhole stitches. Thread with ribbon laces. Add decorative trim such as buttons, flowers, bows, or buckles.

ON YOUR OWN

Now that you are a dollmaker, why not get to know others who share your same interest? There are dollmakers the world over. Some work in cloth, others in wood, clay, or fibers, but all share an exuberance for dolls and dollmaking and are happy to share their enthusiasm with others. There are many clubs and organizations for dollmakers. Most towns have a local doll club that welcomes beginners as well as experienced crafters. Neighborhood doll supply stores, fabric stores, and crafting centers are all good references for these local groups.

Magazines, catalogs, and journals will keep you abreast of dollmaking news. Nationally distributed newsletters like the one from the Association of People Who Play with Dolls are filled with patterns, crafting hints, and announcements of classes and doll exhibits.

National and international dollmaking exhibitions and seminars, such as the annual conference of the National Institute of American Doll Artists, Doll Makers Magic, and the biannual Doll University, sponsored by the National Cloth Doll Makers Association, provide a terrific opportunity for getting to know the experts in the field and making friends with other dollmakers. Nothing will fan your own creative fires like the camaraderie and creative exchange with others who are also pursuing their love of sewing and sculpting dolls.

CONCLUSION

Information, inspiration, and confidence—I hope you have gained all of these and more from this book. The reward of mastering the basics is your ability to sew and sculpt dolls of unlimited artistry and imagination. All the characters that live within your imagination can spring to life once you have the skill and the means for realizing their creation.

I want to share some of my recent imaginings that have sprung to life through the artistry of polymer clay, cloth, and wood. I do confess that I pulled a few strings to make this happen! I have always loved the magical enchantment of puppets and marionettes, so it wasn't long before my dollmaking took a new path from sewing cloth dolls to the creation of marionettes. My current crafting proved far more satisfactory than my early childhood efforts of stringing dolls from the rafters of the garage with clothesline and picture wire. I discovered that the fluid motion of even the simplest of screw-eye joints appeared very realistic, and when strung and suspended in animated gestures, each doll character seemed to have a spirit all its own. Designs of polymer clay, wooden dowels and blocks, cloth, and assemblages of oddities, such as rusty sardine tins, old bed springs, and junk jewelry, soon filled my studio.

Your dollmaking will also progress down its own special path. Preferences in materials and processes, special interests such as pastimes or particular places, and the discovery of your own marvelous skills and talents will all play a part in determining your dollmaking direction. It is exciting to think of all the possibilities! What new dollmaking avenues will you explore? What new doll characters will you bring to life? Whatever road you take, I wish you a journey filled with happy discovery and the many creative challenges that come from sewing and sculpting dolls.

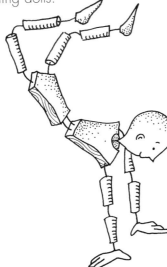

It is easy to transform your polymer and cloth Medley Dolls into dainty marionettes. The large sprite pictured here has a jointed wooden body substituted for the cloth torso. Her polymer clay head, hands, and feet are attached to the body with screw-eyes that are imbedded into the clay before it is baked. Strings are attached to strategically placed screw-eyes and through small holes in the hands. Her wee companion is sculpted entirely of polymer clay and has screw-eye joints covered and bound together with twine that matches her skin tone.

The school girl's white polymer clay head, hands, and feet are first colored with fabric pens and then rebaked to adhere the pigment permanently to the clay. The clay pieces are then attached to a wooden body and dressed in specially designed clothing which allows the joints to move freely. A small red apple, once a holiday ornament, and a tiny address book have been transformed into the diminutive school accessories. Keep an eye out for interesting small-scale items that will add the perfect final accent to each of your doll projects.

INDEX

ABOUT THE AUTHOR

Eloise Piper received a Bachelor of Fine Arts degree from Carnegie Mellon University and a Masters in Art Education from the University of Pittsburgh. She taught art in the Pittsburgh Public Schools, developed the art curriculum for their Preprimary program, and served as supervising art consultant for the program. She presented Head Start training classes at Carnegie Mellon University and at Pennsylvania State University. She also taught crafts at the Western Pennsylvania School for the Deaf and gave batik workshops at numerous craft schools and art centers. She has been a faculty member at National University and at the University of San Diego, where she taught sculpture, drawing, composition, and art appreciation.

Ellie is a painter whose work can be found in major corporate and residential collections here and abroad. Her batik work is documented in the slide collection at New York City's Cooper-Hewitt Museum. She received the Mrs. Clifford S. Heinz award at the Carnegie Museum of Art, purchase prizes from Pittsburgh's One Hundred Friends of Art, and first prize in a National Craft Council exhibit. Her numerous solo exhibits include a retrospective show while Artist-in-Residence at the Indiana University of Pennsylvania and a traveling exhibition of batik paintings sponsored by Baltimore's Museum Without Walls. She participated in the Bicentennial Barge exhibition and was included in the Ten Women Artists of Allegheny County exhibit. Her work has been reproduced in Herbick and Held's Calendar of Artists, *Craft Horizons* magazine, and *Pittsburgh Magazine*. Her other books include *Creating and Crafting Dolls* (Chilton Book Company, 1993) and *Fresh Flowers* (Matthew Thomas Designs, 1990).

Ellie lives in San Diego, California. When she is not busy painting, writing, dollmaking, or presenting workshops, she can be found working in her garden or visiting her two daughters and three granddaughters, all of whom share her love of dolls.